IN SPITE OF HANDICAPS

RALPH W. BULLOCK

IN SPITE OF HANDICAPS

BRIEF BIOGRAPHICAL SKETCHES WITH DISCUSSION OUTLINES OF OUTSTANDING NEGROES NOW LIVING WHO ARE ACHIEVING DISTINCTION IN VARIOUS LINES OF ENDEAVOR

RALPH W. BULLOCK
BOYS' WORK SECRETARY, NATIONAL COUNCIL Y M C A

With a Foreword by Channing H. Tobias
Senior Secretary, Colored Work Department
National Council Y M C A

Essay Index Reprint Series

BOOKS FOR LIBRARIES PRESS
FREEPORT, NEW YORK

First Published 1927
Reprinted 1968

INTERNATIONAL STANDARD BOOK NUMBER:
0-8369-0264-5

LIBRARY OF CONGRESS CATALOG CARD NUMBER:
68-25602

PRINTED IN THE UNITED STATES OF AMERICA

ACKNOWLEDGMENT

WHEN one attempts to portray the character, personality and achievements of others through the medium of biographical sketches he soon finds himself engaged in one of the most difficult forms of writing. The writer always finds himself handicapped by the limits of his experience and his knowledge of others. Therefore, he is compelled to seek the aid of friends. This little volume owes much to the generous help of friends throughout the country in securing and compiling information and data concerning the persons whose life sketches have been used. I am indebted to the characters of this book for their kindness in allowing the stories of their lives to be used for this purpose. Gratitude is due Dr. Channing H. Tobias for reading the manuscripts, and the many helpful suggestions offered by him. I am also deeply indebted to Mr. Abel J. Gregg for his counsel and help in preparing the discussion outlines accompanying the story sketches. In submitting this volume to the public it is hoped that it will serve the purpose of inspiring youth to worthwhile achievements in life and at the same time help it to develop attitudes of interracial good will, that peace and happiness may dwell among them.

R. W. BULLOCK
Boys' Work Secretary
National Council Y M C A

CONTENTS

	PAGE
ROLAND HAYES.....................*Music–soloist*	1
MORDECAI WYATT JOHNSON..........*Minister–orator*	7
ROBERT RUSSA MOTON..........*Educator–industrial*	15
CHARLES CLINTON SPAULDING...............*Business*	23
COUNTÉE CULLEN...........................*Poet*	29
HARRY T. BURLEIGH...............*Music–composer*	35
GEORGE WASHINGTON CARVER..............*Scientist*	45
DANIEL HALE WILLIAMS....................*Surgeon*	53
DEHART HUBBARD.........................*Athlete*	59
WILLIAM EDWARD BURGHARDT DUBOIS..*Author-editor*	67
JOHN HOPE....................*Educator–collegiate*	73
ARCHIE ALPHONSO ALEXANDER........*Civil Engineer*	79
MATTHEW W. BULLOCK......................*Law*	85
HENRY OSSAWA TANNER....................*Painter*	91
JAMES WELDON JOHNSON..............*Author–poet*	97
MARY MCLEOD BETHUNE.....*Educator—club leader*	103
MAX YERGAN..........................*Missionary*	111
CARTER G. WOODSON.....................*Historian*	121
BIBLIOGRAPHY	131

FOREWORD

FROM time to time requests have come to the offices of the National Council of the Y M C A for a book of brief biographical sketches of Negroes who are achieving distinction along business, professional, and artistic lines. Most of these requests have come from leaders of white boys' and girls' clubs who desired to promote better interracial understanding, and leaders of colored groups who desired to stimulate the race pride of colored youth. In preparing the sketches in this book the author, who is National Boys' Work Secretary of the Y M C A, has had especially these two groups in mind. In selecting the subjects an effort has been made to choose one outstanding representative of each of the principal professions or lines of work in which Negroes have distinguished themselves. In one or two instances persons of the same profession have been chosen because each has distinguished himself in a different phase of the profession.

For the convenience of discussion groups a question outline follows each sketch, and a carefully selected bibliography of books about the Negro and books by Negro authors is given at the close of the book.

If white youth through reading these sketches gain a fuller knowledge of and higher respect for Negroes, and colored youth are led to a deeper sense of self-respect and pride in the achievements of their kind, the book will have served its purpose.

Channing H. Tobias,
Senior Secretary, Colored Work Department
National Council of the Y M C A
New York City, 1927

ROLAND HAYES

ROLAND HAYES

ROLAND HAYES was born thirty-eight years ago in Curryville, Ga., a little cluster of huts that was not even a village, located several miles from the nearest railroad. His mother, to whom he ascribes his success, was a "wonderful woman with wisdom and great understanding." When her sons were very young she moved to Chattanooga, Tenn., in order that her boys might have an opportunity to go to school.

"While we were waiting for school to open," says Hayes, "I found a job in a factory that made window weights. It was the hardest work that I have ever done. I had to unload pig iron, handle the rough scrap iron, help charge the cupolas with wood and coke, and with another man carry the heavy ladles brimming with melted iron to pour into the moulds for casting the window weights. I wore old shoes that had no laces in them so that I could kick them off more easily when the hot iron would spill. My feet are peppered now with scars where the hot flakes of iron fell on them."

At the age of seventeen, Hayes met Arthur Calhoun, an Oberlin music student, who induced him to try training his voice, but his mother distrusted "dance-hall singers," the only kind she knew of his race who made any money. But she finally acquiesced and Hayes started in search of an education with his share of the family savings, fifty dollars, in his pocket.

He tried giving church concerts on a "fifty-fifty" basis for a while but his earnings were so small that he decided to give this up. Finally he worked his way to Nashville, Tenn., and by some miracle got into Fisk University, working his way through the four years.

While in school Hayes worked in Louisville, Ky., in the Pendennis Club during the summer months. It was there that his voice won him the added job of entertainer and in that way he attracted Henry H. Putnam, of Boston, Mass. Mr. Putnam interested Hayes in going to Boston for further study. Soon he and his mother were living in Boston, Hayes gave small recitals and studied at the New England Conservatory of Music and finally astonished the world with his first Symphony Hall recital.

This recital was the very first appearance of any Negro musician in that great auditorium. When Roland Hayes, tenor, announced his intention of singing in Boston Symphony Hall, he was laughed at and his friends openly voiced their fears that he could never fill the hall.

The night of the recital came and with it the crowds —and then more crowds, pushing and piling into Symphony Hall with a desperate eagerness to get inside that seemed quite foreign to the accustomed dignity of Boston's center of music. When the moment arrived for the opening there was not an inch of standing room on the floor, balcony, or platform of the great auditorium. For even on the platform, with only a narrow space left for the singer, seats had been packed in row on row, to accommodate the added scores who simply refused to be turned away.

And at the end of the concert, that living mass of humanity refused to dissolve. With applause that increased in volume beyond anything that Symphony Hall was used to, they demanded encores until the singer, in sheer weariness, turned for the last time from the stage and left them huddled still in admiration and joy over the great treat which had been theirs.

"After that," says Hayes, "many things happened. I was beginning to make something of a reputation. A man wrote from Santa Monica, Calif., and the result was a concert out there. After it was over a man from the audience came up to the platform and said: 'I have heard all of the world's most famous singers, but when I listen to you I get something more than I get from their singing. What is it?' I couldn't answer the question myself then, but that night I began to question myself. Could it be something that was given to my forebears, some heritage from the beginning of my race? And, if I could help my race to give this special contribution to the sum of all human contributions to life, was not that my mission? Was that not why I was put on earth? I found that night the clue by which my life was being directed."

Soon Hayes found himself leaving for Europe to study under the old masters. This gave him an opportunity to give concerts in the music centers of Europe. Then came his epoch-making success, taking the continent by storm with his interpretations of the Negro spirituals. His return to America each year is marked by triumphal processions through the country singing the spirituals and the best songs of many foreign nations. He has mastered French, German, Spanish, and Italian, and sings the songs of other countries in the language in which they were originally written.

Today Roland Hayes stands as one of the greatest lyric tenors on the concert stage, and one of the great singers of all time.

The message of his life is a message of a mission. Hayes felt himself, and still feels himself, called to give to the world through his voice, the expression of the throbbing heart of a race. He feels within himself the God-sent urge to interpret in song the life of his own people and with a fixed purpose to accomplish this urge he goes steadily on to his ever-increasing success.

In 1924, Mr. Hayes was awarded the Spingarn Medal which is given every year under the direction of the National Association for the Advancement of Colored People to the Negro who makes the greatest contribution to the advancement of his race. For the same year, his receipts from his recitals and concerts exceeded one hundred thousand dollars. But he is not overcome by that which seems to be material success. He counts as his highest achievement the interpretation of the inner life of his race to the world.

ROLAND HAYES

1. List the difficulties which Roland Hayes faced in his desire to become a good musician.

2. Were his difficulties more or less than those the average Negro boy faces? Average white boy? Why do you believe as you do?

3. Should colored boys with possibilities such as Hayes has demonstrated be given even chances, or given better chances than the average white boy? Why do you believe as you do?

4. What do you think of Hayes' idea that the Negro race may have a musical gift to make to humankind which is superior to that of any other race?

5. Should Hayes be encouraged or discouraged in his life mission of "helping my race to give this special contribution to the sum of all human contributions to life"? Why?

6. In a concert hall where Negroes were given less desirable seats than white people, Hayes protested against the discrimination. Should he be encouraged or discouraged in such protests? Why?

7. What other situations will Hayes have to overcome if he realizes his mission and helps Negroes to superior places of prominence in musical contributions? List them.

8. In which of these situations can groups such as this play a helpful part?

9. Just what would this group need to do if it is really to help?

MORDECAI WYATT JOHNSON

MORDECAI WYATT JOHNSON

THE story of the life of Mordecai Wyatt Johnson is one of continuous effort blended with successful achievement. He was born Jan. 12, 1890, at Paris, Tenn., the son of Rev. Wyatt J. Johnson and Mrs. Carolyn Freeman Johnson.

Fortunately for him, he lived near a public school which he attended until his graduation from the eighth grade in 1903. This gave him an early start in life, and he has made use of every succeeding opportunity for intellectual development, until now he is recognized among America's leading thinkers.

Johnson's educational career has been somewhat transitory, yet consistent. In the fall of 1903 he entered the high-school department of Roger Williams University in Nashville, Tenn., and continued his studies there until the winter of 1904-1905 when the school was burned. He then went to Howe Institute, Memphis, Tenn., for the remainder of that school term. In the fall of 1905 he entered Morehouse College, graduating from this institution in 1911 with the Bachelor of Arts degree. Because of his high scholastic standing as a college student he was retained by the College as Professor of English in the high-school department for the year 1911-1912. He immediately took up his studies at the University of Chicago during the summer months—concentrating on the social sciences. For the school year of 1912-1913 he taught Economics and History at Morehouse College. In 1913 he received a Bachelor's degree from the University of Chicago for the work which he had done there in the summer school.

In the fall of 1913 Dr. Johnson gave up his work as a teacher and entered Rochester Theological Seminary. While studying at Rochester he became pastor of the Second Baptist Church at Mumford, N. Y., which pastorate he held until his graduation from the seminary in 1916. The degree, Bachelor of Divinity, was given to him by the Rochester Seminary in 1921 for the presentation of a thesis entitled, "The Rise of the Knights Templars."

In 1916 Dr. Johnson was selected by the International Committee of the Y M C A as Student Secretary to fill the place left vacant by Max Yergan in the southwestern field. While serving in this capacity he made a careful study of the Negro schools and colleges in the southwestern territory and recommended the formation of the Southwestern Annual Student Conference, which has had continual growth in both size and effectiveness since its organization. After serving with the Y M C A for six months he received a letter from Dr. John R. Mott notifying him that the International Committee had taken special notice of his work and had voted to raise his salary immediately. Notwithstanding the raise in salary and Dr. Mott's indicating that there was a large future ahead of him in Y M C A work, Dr. Johnson followed his "urge" to preach, and in 1917 he entered the pastorate of the First Baptist Church, Charleston, W. Va.

While serving in this capacity not only did Dr. Johnson furnish spiritual leadership for his congregation and build up a powerful church organization but he became the leading spirit in the social and economic life of the colored people of Charleston. During the eight years of his pastorate in Charleston he also became widely known throughout the country as an outstanding pulpit orator with a social gospel which challenges men to the *Christ* way of life.

Dr. Johnson's participation in civic and community enterprises reflects his training in sociology and economics while at the University of Chicago. Very soon after moving to West Virginia he was selected chairman of the Auxiliary County Council Defense. As chairman of this body he conducted the World War Finance Campaign for Kanawha County, W. Va.

After the close of the World War when more time could be given to the development of racial interest he organized the Charleston Branch of the National Association for the Advancement of Colored People, and before leaving Charleston in 1926 he had brought the membership of this organization up to 1,000.

With interest growing ever deeper in the community welfare of his people Dr. Johnson organized the Commercial Cooperative Society in Charleston and established the Cooperative Cash Grocery, a Rochedale cooperative store among colored people. This organization is now under the management of Jordan P. Tinsley and is in its fifth year of existence as a thriving business concern.

Reaching out beyond local community boundaries, Dr. Johnson reorganized the finances of the West Virginia Baptist State Convention, bringing the total receipts of the General Convention and the Women's Convention in one year from $5,900 to $14,000.

While the above statements regarding Dr. Johnson's community activities in West Virginia are rather pointed, and perhaps lacking in interest, one must admit that they are indicative of the large service which a minister and pastor may render his people when fully prepared for his task of leadership.

Dr. Johnson secured a leave of absence from his pastorate in 1921 and entered Harvard University for a year's graduate work. In June of 1922 he received from Harvard the degree of Master of the Science of Theology. Because of the splendid scholastic record which he made during his year's study at Harvard he was selected as one of the Commencement speakers, delivering as the graduate commencement part an address entitled, "The Faith of the American Negro." This address was reprinted in *The Crisis* and in *The Nation*. It is also included in Carter G. Woodson's book entitled "Negro Orators and Their Orations."

Something more of Dr. Johnson's power as a pulpit orator and public speaker may be understood when we recall that in 1925-1926 he was selected as a member

MORDECAI WYATT JOHNSON

of the Sherwood Eddy party on Community-wide Social Evangelism in Des Moines, Iowa, and in Atlanta, Ga. His gripping social messages drew large gatherings of white and colored people in both Des Moines and Atlanta. In the summer of 1926 he was a member of the Sherwood Eddy American Seminar, traveling and studying in Europe. While in Europe with Eddy's party on June 30 he was elected to the Presidency of Howard University. He assumed this new office Sept. 1, 1926, and has served admirably until the present writing.

In commenting further upon Dr. Johnson's power as a public speaker it is interesting and sufficient to quote from an article in the March issue of the *Opportunity* magazine, written by Mrs. Anne Biddle Stirling (white) in which she writes:

The American Friends Service Committee recently held in Washington, D. C., a two-day conference on Interracial Relations, to which were asked certain southern and northern friends and colored people.

The evening session of the first day was to hear from the Reverend Mordecai Johnson, the new president of Howard University. I had heard many of the leading Negroes of America: Booker T. Washington, Robert R. Moton, John Hope, Kelly Miller, Dr. George Cannon, W. E. B. DuBois, Leslie P. Hill and a lot of other lights; this was a man unknown to me. I gave close attention.

He opened his mouth and I yielded myself to the charm of the deep mellow voice that is the Negro's heritage. With psychological skill in handling his audience, he prefaced his address by counting up the points of unity between himself and the Quakers. Then he traced the difficulty between our races back to its economic sources.

He was saying things in a new way. Eyes met in pleased surprise. These were new pastures—pencils scribbled busily.

Presently tears came, were dashed away to clear my gaze on this protean speaker and yet kept coming; I strove to keep from visibly shaking.

Puzzled by my unusual emotion, I interrupted my fascinated gaze to turn appraising eyes on the row behind me: one met my eyes in sympathetic smile; all the other eyes were fixed on the speaker.

Presently that rich voice—sometimes booming in thunderous denunciation, sometimes persuading in softest sympathy—ceased, and vibrant silence covered us.

A veteran apostle in this race field said to me huskily: "I have never heard an address to match it." My next-door neighbor said: "These people will never forget what they heard tonight. For years to come some phrase will suddenly grip them!"

In the waking watches of that night I tried to analyze what seemed like wizardry. What was, whence came the power of this man who played on our heart strings as if they were harp strings with never a jarring chord! Silent hours spent in searching *Why* seemed to bring this answer: Seldom do we meet a spirit so Christ-like in pity for poor sinners. This is not the first time we have had our souls hung up before us and the thin places and smudges pointed out, but never before with such sincerity and comprehension of the struggle involved, such sympathy for the weakness of the honest striving soul.

This man, too, has borne his cross for weary years of

abnegation and it has taught him an almost divine compassion for all the world. Not for a moment did his compassion soften the force of his stentorian scorn of the hypocrite. Mentally I see him still—sartorially correct and unaware—leaning forward over the rail, gentle of voice, impeccable of diction, smiling persuasively—suddenly spring erect, seemingly to add inches to his stature, his coaxing eyes blazing widely as he roared his wrath at the harm and wrong done by the creeping coward, who, with his mouth cried, "Lord! Lord!" while in his life he doeth not the will of the Master.

One reading the above story who has never heard Dr. Johnson speak perhaps will feel that the picture is somewhat overdrawn, but all of those who have heard him will agree that it is a fair appraisal of him as a public speaker. His addresses, both here in America and in Europe have been far-reaching in effect.

Reviewing carefully the life of Dr. Johnson we must admit that he laid well his foundation for life and while yet a young man his achievement has been great, with no lost motion in his career since he first entered the public schools of Paris, Tenn.

MORDECAI WYATT JOHNSON

1. What handicaps do Negroes face, as they struggle to make a contribution to life today, which white men do not face?

2. If a Negro and a white man were both struggling to make the sort of contribution Mordecai Johnson is making, would the Negro have to be less capable, equally capable,

or more capable in order to make the same contribution the white man did? Why do you believe as you do?

3. How would Mordecai Johnson measure up with the leading ministers in America today?

4. How do you account for the contribution which Mordecai Johnson has and is making?

    a. From what sources in his experience did he develop that plus personality which gives him his place of leadership today?

    b. What attitude does he seem to have taken toward study? How was he rated as a student?

    c. What characteristics of his work, in the Y M C A and in his pastorate, throw light on his method of personal development?

5. To what extent is the pathway Johnson has followed open to other Negro and white boys?

6. Is it or is it not worth while to develop oneself so as to be able to make the contribution Johnson is making?

7. What would a desire to follow Johnson's pathway demand of a boy? In his studies? In his home? In relation to his race? In relation to his knowledge of conditions in America today?

ROBERT RUSSA MOTON

AMERICAN educational theory acknowledges a debt to Negro educators who have worked out the formula of systematic industrial training. Two Negro institutions, Hampton and Tuskegee, stand as monuments to that branch of educational thought; one man, Robert Russa Moton, carries on today the tradition of both schools.

Educated at Hampton, for twenty-five years the center of Hampton life and the head of its program, planning and developing its ever-widening sphere of influence, Robert Russa Moton came to represent the Hampton idea in the public mind.

When, with the death of Booker T. Washington, founder of Tuskegee, a successor for his position in the Alabama school was sought, Robert Moton was chosen, and today he stands as completely identified with Tuskegee and the Tuskegee idea as he has been with his Virginia institution. He has been ten years at Tuskegee. His influence was largely responsible for uniting the two schools in a successful $7,000,000 endowment campaign.

Dr. Moton's life traces itself back into the dim drabness of slavery and a slave plantation. He was born in Amelia County, Va., Aug. 26, 1867, the son of

Booker Moton and Emily Brown. His mother was a cook in the "big house" of the white "master"; his father led the field hands in their daily tasks.

Among Moton's earliest recollections are scenes on the Virginia plantation, where the boy followed his "mistress" around, carrying her basket of keys. As soon as he was able, and according to the rigorous slave code, even sooner, he was called upon to assist with the chores about the yard. Even after starting to school, young Moton filled in his few free hours as small "handy man" for this same family.

A story which has been often repeated is told by Moton himself as marking a turning point in his career. One of the young boys on the plantation had become a playmate and a close friend of the little chore boy. They remained constantly in as close contact and as free intimacy as was possible under such a social system.

A parting of the ways came when the white boy was sent away for his education, to Virginia Polytechnic Institute. The year that his playmate was in school dragged slowly by for Moton, but he looked forward to the boy's return with keen anticipation, expecting to sit through more than one long evening under the Virginia sky while his former "buddy" related the wonders of school life and the thrills of school experience.

The vacation period came and the boy came back. But there was no hand-shaking at the old plantation house; there were no warm greetings between the two boys, and after this shock of the first meeting young

Moton knew that all hope of any long evenings of intimate companionship must take flight. For his erstwhile companion greeted him with the coldest of nods and a manner as frigid as the north wind. But to Moton's mother, the old cook, he flashed a warm welcome, threw his arms about her, and embraced her.

The experience, it is told, "sent young Moton out through the darkness, down the ravine, across the valley, and up to their cabin on the hill. He slept but little that night, and arose early the next morning, more weary than when he had gone to bed," but with one fixed determination: he would get for himself the same education of which the white boy boasted.

He worked two years in a Surrey County lumber camp, then offered himself for entrance examinations at Hampton, at the age of eighteen. He failed, but was offered a job in the kitchen, on the farm, or in the saw mill. He chose the saw mill, and for twelve months worked there while attending night school. He was finally admitted to the day school, and finished the prescribed course in four years.

Immediately after being graduated, he was sought by the school to be its assistant commandant in charge of the male students, both Indians and Negroes. Hardly had Moton been in the position a year when the commandant resigned, and General Armstrong, the principal of the institution, offered Moton his place, despite common assertions that "Negroes would not study under a Negro." So thoroughly did Moton's régime explode that bogey, that although he had intended to stay only two years, he was induced to remain at his post, and a quarter of a century passed while he labored in the service of Hampton.

With the death of General Armstrong, increased responsibility fell upon the young commandant. The whole intricate network of problems involved in the relationships of the two races in the South as affected Hampton was now his to handle. Gradually the United States government withdrew its Indian students from Hampton, and the school became an entirely Negro school.

As guide, counsellor, and teacher of his race at Hampton, Moton spread his influence throughout the southland. In Virginia he was known through the Negro organization society, and in other states he was to the Negroes and whites alike the "friend and counsellor of Booker Washington."

He has played a leading part in the work of the Negro Business League of which he is now president, and has been drawn into other nation-wide movements for the benefit of the race.

He has been honored with honorary degrees from several universities. Williams College in 1920 gave him the LL.D. degree, as had Oberlin and Virginia Union. Lincoln University bestowed the same degree five years ago.

In 1908 he was made secretary of the Jeanes rural school fund board. He is trustee of the People's village school at Mt. Meigs, Ala.; of the Industrial Home School for Colored Girls at Peak, Va.; of the Negro

Reform School for Boys at Hanover, Va.; of Fisk University at Nashville, Tenn.; he is vice-chairman of the National League on Urban Conditions among Negroes, and president of the National Negro Business League. He is a member of the executive committee of the Permanent Roosevelt Memorial movement, and of the National Child Welfare Association; and was made a member of the International Committee of the Y M C A in 1919. Among his writings have been "Finding a Way Out," his autobiography, "Racial Good Will," and numerous contributions to magazines.

During the period of the World War, Dr. Moton was instrumental in negotiating a loan of $5,000,000 from the United States government for use in Liberia. He was also very active in speaking to the people on many tours in the interest of War Savings Stamps, Liberty Loan drives, and the conservation of food.

The spirit of Dr. Moton is shown very clearly in the following extract from the autobiography of his life, "Finding a Way Out":

In order that this institution shall continue to carry forward the ideals of its great founder, in order that it shall not cease to render large service to humankind, in order that we shall keep the respect and confidence of the people of this land, we must, first, every one of us—principal, officers, teachers, graduates and students—use every opportunity and strive in every reasonable way to strengthen and develop between white and black people, North and South, that unselfish cooperation which has characterized the Tuskegee Institute from its beginning. Second, we must patiently and persistently in the spirit of unselfish devotion follow the methods of education which in this school have been so distinctive, so unique, and so helpful. Third, we must consecrate and reconsecrate our lives to this work as instruments in God's hands for the training of black men and women for service, in whatever capacity, or in whatever locality they may find human need. Fourth, there must be no cantankerousness here—we must all work absolutely together.

ROBERT RUSSA MOTON

1. Read over again the incident of Moton's experience with his white boy playmate.
2. Does a real friendship seem to exist between the two boys on the plantation? What evidence leads you to believe as you do?
3. Was it natural and just for Moton to look forward to the return of his white boy friend? Why do you believe as you do?
4. How do you account for the change in the white boy's attitude toward Moton upon his return from school?
    a. Just what influences might have caused that change? List them.
    b. To what extent can each of them be justified?
    c. From Moton's point of view which ones can be justified?
5. What happens in the heart of a boy when he is treated as Moton was treated?
6. If all boys, white and colored, alike, were to undergo similar treatment would the results be good or bad for the races as a whole? Why?

7. To what extent was the white boy to blame? Wherein was he helpless? What should he have done?

8. What are boys to do when they are caught as Moton and his white boy friend were caught?

    a. What do you think of Moton's resolve?

    b. Is or is not that course of action open to all boys so caught?

9. What can colored and white boys do to overcome the forces which cause these broken friendships? What things could they do together? What things could clubs do together?

CHARLES CLINTON SPAULDING

CHARLES CLINTON SPAULDING

FROM plowboy to president of a two and a quarter million dollar corporation is the story of the career of Charles Clinton Spaulding, president of the institution which he built up through years of patient work in a section where only distrust of Negro business enterprises had formerly prevailed.

Born on a small North Carolina farm, he manages today the largest going insurance company within the race, a company which paid $729,833 to policy holders last year while increasing its surplus to an amount exceeding $100,000. The company maintains an agency force of 450 workers in twelve states, with headquarters in its $250,000 modern, seven-story office building in Durham, N. C.

Charles Clinton Spaulding was born in Clarkton, N. C., Aug. 1, 1874. As soon as he was old enough to do a day's work in the field he was sent out with the rest of the boys to take his turn at the plow. But dissatisfaction with the dull routine of farm life early manifested itself, and at an early age he sought permission to join an uncle who was a graduate of the Leonard Medical College, and was then practicing in Durham, N. C.

The late Dr. A. M. Moore was the uncle. Young

Spaulding joined him in Durham and his first job was as a dishwasher in a Durham hotel for $10 a month. He was soon promoted to head bellboy, and then side waiter, but finding that he could not attend school while holding down these jobs, he took a position as a cook for Judge R. W. Winston whom he served for two years while going to school.

Upon graduation from the Whitted graded school in 1898 he accepted a job as manager of a grocery company into which twenty-five of Durham's leading colored citizens had put $10 each. The company got into financial straits, the other members withdrew their investment, and Spaulding was left with bare shelves and a $300 indebtedness. It took him five years to work out of it.

Just at this time Dr. Moore and John Merrick decided to make a second effort to launch an insurance company, and Spaulding was called in to help. With such funds as they could spare he managed the company, while serving as office boy, janitor, agent, and manager. He sold all the policies, collected all the premiums, and kept the records. Out of his travels over the state grew the structure of the North Carolian Mutual Life Insurance company, founded in 1898.

Last year the company collected more than $2,000,000 in income. Its balance sheet shows assets of $300,000 in real estate, $900,000 in first mortgages to Negroes on real estate valued at more than $2,000,000, more than $200,000 in policy loans, and

$350,000 in approved stocks and bonds. The cash item is $100,000.

Examiners of the insurance departments of three states have concurred in a report that the North Carolina Mutual Life Insurance Company is the only mutual life insurance company of any size in the entire state of North Carolina which is managed and owned exclusively by and for its policy holders.

Under President Spaulding are Dr. Clyde Donnell, medical director, E. R. Merrick, treasurer, J. M. Avery, vice-president, and R. L. MacDougald, vice-president, all of whom are members of the company's board of directors.

Mr. Spaulding has mapped out a program of social service which stretches far beyond the ordinary routine functions of a business corporation. Employment is provided for hundreds, while, through its control of capital, it has been able, within the limits of safe investment and of sound financial policy, to finance the building of homes, the development of industries, and the general uplift of the race.

The organization of the medical department under Mr. Spaulding includes at the home office a morbidity, mortality, and life-extension service, while in the field a staff of 500 workers cooperate in the prevention of disease and premature death.

The life of Charles Clinton Spaulding tells a story of grim perseverance that lifted a boy from plow hand on a farm to the presidency of a giant industry, simply because he refused to be downed. When his grocery venture failed and left him with a $300 indebtedness, he simply gathered himself together, started over again, and used the failure as a new point of departure for a career that was to prove far more remunerative and socially useful than his success as a grocery man could possibly have been.

CHARLES CLINTON SPAULDING

1. What were some of the difficulties which Mr. Spaulding encountered in his business career?

2. How does Spaulding's progress in business compare with that of other business men of today whose beginning was similar to his?

3. Wherein was Mr. Spaulding at advantage or at disadvantage as compared with the average Negro? The average white man?

4. To what extent should Negro business men such as Spaulding be given an opportunity to develop their business among other races just as white business men do?

5. What difficulties did Mr. Spaulding have which white business men never face?

6. What justifies a law forbidding Negroes to sell white people insurance and yet does not restrict white insurance companies from soliciting Negro business?

7. How can social conditions be so changed as to allow Negro business men, such as Spaulding, an opportunity to develop their business among all races here in America?

8. What can we do as individuals and as a group to help change conditions so that Negro business men will have as much freedom in promoting their business among other races as white men have?

9. What would the ethics of Jesus require in this matter?
10. Just what would happen if Jesus' ethics were applied to the situation the Negro business man faces in America today?

COUNTEE CULLEN

COUNTÉE CULLEN

COUNTÉE CULLEN was born in New York City in 1903 and is the adopted son of Rev. F. A. Cullen, Minister of Salem M. E. Church. He was educated in the public schools of New York City, DeWitt Clinton High School from which he was graduated in 1922, and New York University, from which he was graduated in June, 1925, receiving the degree of Bachelor of Arts. He was elected to the Phi Beta Kappa Society in March, 1925. In the fall of 1925 he entered Harvard University and received the degree of Master of Arts in June, 1926, concentrating on English literature.

Cullen began to write when he was fourteen years of age. George Cronyn, a teacher at DeWitt Clinton High School, had a theory that high school students could write verse. He gave an assignment to his class and Cullen did as an assignment, and not because he had any idea of ever writing poetry the only free-verse poem he has ever done, a verse entitled "To a Swimmer." He thought no more of writing until a year later when he saw this poem published in the May, 1918, issue of *The Modern School Magazine*. He then became ambitious to write and his first verse appeared in *The Crisis*, a magazine published by the National Association for the Advancement of Colored People. While at DeWitt Clinton High School he was awarded first prize in a contest conducted by the Federation of Women's Clubs with his poem, "I have a Rendezvous with Life." Cullen entered his poem "Heritage" in the 1925 contest of the Poetry Society, this being the last year that he was eligible for participation as he graduated in June of that year.

In November, 1923, he published his verse, "To a Brown Boy," which appeared in *The Bookman*. In 1924 he published poems in *The Bookman, Harper's, The American Mercury, The Century, The Nation, Poetry, Opportunity, Messenger,* and several other publications. The first collection of these poems, "Color," was published in October, 1925, by Harper and Brothers. In 1925 he published verse in *The Survey, Graphic,* and *Harper's*. His poems have been reprinted in The New York *Tribune, The Literary Digest,* The New York *World* and several other newspapers. Perhaps his most widely quoted verse is the epitaph, "To a Lady I Know," which reads:

> She even thinks that up in heaven
> Her class lies late and snores,
> While poor black cherubs rise at **seven**
> To do celestial chores.

When Cullen first began to write he was very much influenced by and was a great admirer of Tennyson. Tennyson has since been supplanted by Edna St. Vincent Millay, Housman, Robinson, and Keats. Cullen is essentially an emotional and lyrical poet. His only present tendency towards free verse is in experimental attempts, and he finds himself more and more inclined toward the more rigid forms. "Most things I write," he says, "I do for the sheer love of the music in them. A number of times I have said I wanted to be a poet and known as such, and not as a Negro poet. Somehow or other, however, I find my poetry of itself treating of the Negro, of his joys and his sorrows—mostly of the latter—and of the heights and depths of emotion which I feel as a Negro."

Witter Bynner, who has been a sincere friend and adviser of Cullen, said in a letter to him in June, 1924: "You are very young and have suddenly developed your gift as a poet out of the mediocre into the distinguished." Laurence Stallings in the New York *World* of Jan. 7, 1925, while summing up the contents for the year of *The American Mercury,* made the statement that the only distinguished verse that appeared in that magazine during 1924 was "The Shroud of Color" by Mr. Cullen, which appeared in the November issue.

In 1924, Cullen won the second prize in the contest held by the Poetry Society of America with a poem, "The Ballad of the Brown Girl." There were seven hundred competitors from sixty-three colleges. This was the second time that Cullen took the second prize in this contest.

The early success of Cullen has been hailed by critics as the beginning of a revival movement in Negro literary production. Many of the keenest students of American writings look to Cullen and to the school of writing which he represents, to bring the Negro to the forefront in the field of poetry. They think of Cullen as a leader in the present-day renaissance of Negro literature. His life, he himself has described, with characteristic modesty, as "anything but exciting." Boys interested in following the steps of this young writer who has already made America follow with interest his pen, however, may find no little "excitement" in a career that began in high school and has already wound its way through two of this country's most noted universities.

Not only as a writer of thoroughly readable verse, but as a critic of what has been done by others, Countée Cullen has found an audience. Commenting for the New York *Survey* upon the recent release of the University of North Carolina, "The Negro and His Songs," by Howard W. Odum and Guy B. Johnson, Cullen writes: "It is done with a scholarly acumen for detail, and a dispassionate notation on the specimens." Continuing in an analysis of the book in which these southern white professors laid bare their criticism of Negro literary endeavor, Cullen displays a fine appreciative gift of and a firm grip on his subject that reflect genuine scholarship. "Since even the most cultured and emancipated Negro," he writes, "cannot plead absolute dissociation from his southern brother, however fettered, and since these songs are indigenous, root products, chips from the rock out of which the race

COUNTÉE CULLEN

was hewn, they must be taken broadly as an index to the race life with the emphasis on the South. The Negro's inherent tendency to sing at all times, as well as his earnest, heart-and-soul performance, is proverbial; a careful analysis of these songs furnishes light on the race not otherwise to be gotten."

Life is still ahead of young Cullen, whose writings, whether critical or creative, have already attracted the attention of the foremost literary critics and writers. Whether he will fall heir to the mantle of Dunbar, and as the new "poet laureate of a race" bear to heights yet unattained the claim of the Negro to literary greatness, remains to be seen. His early career has shown him master of all the essentials of success. Talent must have been his, or the writings of a pen that must still be held immature could never have attracted nation-wide attention. But far more important, young Cullen shows the willingness to improve his talent by industry, by diligent school work, by constant attention to detail and now, with the first dawning of the success that will probably be his, he displays a modesty that stamps him as what the boys call "a thoroughbred."

COUNTÉE CULLEN

1. What were the steps in Countée Cullen's education?
2. How does it compare with the steps in the education of the average American boy?
3. Should American people be proud or ashamed that

the public-school system of New York has produced a young man of Countée Cullen's capacities?

4. Should they be proud or ashamed if all colored boys and girls were so educated?

5. Why would some people be inclined to regret the fact that Cullen was educated in public schools with white children and graduated with high honors from two of America's best colleges?

6. What attitude should America strive to develop in regard to a common educational system for all its youth? Why?

7. What attitude should America take toward discriminations in its public-school policy which are based on color? Why?

8. Is the use of Jesus' principle, "Love thy neighbor as thyself" practical in regard to public-school education for all American youth?

9. Why is it practicable and workable in New York City?

10. Why has it not been practicable in all of the United States?

11. How can the good example of the New York public-school system be extended?

HARRY T. BURLEIGH

HARRY T. BURLEIGH

IN commenting on the life of Burleigh one writer has said, "If Harry Burleigh's musical gift had been less genuine it might have been smothered out by the difficulties of his life, for this composer-to-be was born and reared in deep poverty, with the added handicap of Negro blood."

But there was a strain of courage and determination, however, in that blood, of which the boy might well be proud. His grandfather, Hamilton Waters, was an escaped slave who became blind as a result of the hardships which he endured in slavery. Yet blind, he worked until he reached a ripe old age, supporting himself and aiding as far as he could his family.

Harry's mother was born near Lansing, Mich., in a wagon in which her parents were trying to make their way into Canada. Perhaps the birth of the baby and the mother's needs caused them to change their plans for they did not cross the border, but turned aside and settled in Erie, Pa.

Here the blind father set himself to provide for his family by setting up in business for himself as a presser of men's clothing. He also secured the job as "town crier," a position not to be obtained nowadays, when an extra paper is printed at any hour of the day that anything unusual happens.

By the time the baby which was born in the wagon had grown up and finished high school, her father was able, by close saving and self-denial to send her to college. Upon graduation she found that no place was open to her to do the work for which she had been prepared. This was before the close of the Civil War, and neither North nor South offered many opportunities for educated Negroes. She married later and became the mother of five children. Henry Thacker was born in 1866 and grew up to be known as Harry T. Burleigh, singer and composer.

Harry's father died while the children were yet very young, and his mother had to become the breadwinner for her family. She secured her first job as janitress of a public school, for which she was poorly paid, and it was all she could do to provide food and scanty clothing for her children. The children were forced to work, too, as soon as they were old enough. Harry sold papers, ran errands and worked at whatever other odd jobs he could find.

During these years, Harry was going to public school, and it was here that it was discovered that he had a voice with great possibilities. Through the interest his teacher took in him, Harry developed a passionate love for music which yielded large returns in later years.

Harry's mother frequently worked for a wealthy lady who often brought to her home many distinguished musical artists for the entertainment of her friends, and his mother would always tell him when a recital was to be given. He would often go with his mother to her work and stand outside even in bitter cold weather and listen to some of the great musicians and artists play and sing. Upon one occasion he barely escaped having pneumonia as a result of standing outside in the snow too long listening to the great artist Joseffy. His mother told her employer about the incident, and after that, to prevent the repetition of such an illness, Harry was given a job on the inside, opening the doors for guests.

Among the many artists whom he heard were Mme. Carreno and Mrs. MacDowell. Harry remembered Mrs. MacDowell, and years afterward she played an important part in his life.

While in public school his voice became known to a number of prominent people. He went to public school until he was twenty years of age, always working hard outside of school hours and during summer vacations. During this time he sang in church choirs on Sundays and in the Jewish Synagogue on Saturdays. He studied stenography and after leaving school he worked as a stenographer until he was twenty-six years of age.

In some way he heard that the National Conservatory of Music in New York City had offered some scholarships, and at once he decided to try to get one of them. He went to New York and sang before a committee of judges in a "try-out." There was some question as to his winning a scholarship, but when he sought out the registrar of the conservatory, he recognized Mrs. MacDowell and gave her a letter of recommendation which Mrs. Russell (the lady for whom his mother worked and in whose home he had listened to the great artists) had written for him. Mrs. MacDowell turned the scale in his favor and during his four years of study was his unfailing friend. She gave him clerical work in her office and helped him in every way possible.

Dvörak, director of the conservatory, became interested in Burleigh and gave him much time outside of class hours. Burleigh played and sang for Dvörak the Negro "Spirituals" and also copied many of his orchestral compositions for him. The melody of these Spirituals made a deep impression on the great composer, who later wove one of them into one of his greatest compositions, the "New World Symphony."

Burleigh worked hard during these four years, developing his voice and learning harmony. But there was always the struggle for food and clothing. The scholarship which he was given covered only his tuition. Odd jobs and chores were still necessities to supply his daily needs. His mother found ways of helping him to some extent, as mothers will do. The first summer after he came to New York he went to Saratoga to work in a hotel; by the next summer his voice was becoming known and he went again to Saratoga, not as a hotel waiter, but as baritone soloist in the Episcopal church.

This marked another milestone in his life, because since that time, while he has worked hard, he has been doing work which he likes and for which he is fitted. Subsequent years have brought him the rewards of efficiency and work well done.

In 1894, when the position of baritone soloist became vacant in St. George's Episcopal church in New York, one of the largest churches in the city, Mr. Burleigh applied for the position. He was the only Negro among the sixty applicants, but he had the voice wanted, and Dr. Rainsford, the rector, and the vestrymen did not allow the color of his skin to prevent him from serving. He has remained a member of this choir for thirty-three years. For twenty-six years he has sung in Temple Emanu-El, one of the largest synagogues in the city. And in both choirs he has rendered the most acceptable service.

As soon as his voice became known he was in demand for concerts and private musicales. Several European tours were arranged for him, and for years his annual vacations were spent abroad, where he sang in England and on the continent with great and increasing success. He sang for King Edward VII, and for many of the crowned heads of Europe, who greatly admired his voice.

He has composed the music for about two hundred songs and several festival anthems for choruses, and he has written the scores for a volume of Negro Spirituals. But it is as a singer that he classified himself. " 'Composer,' " he says, when his musical works are spoken of, "Oh, no, just a few songs I've done, and practically no orchestration. My life has been spent as a singer—is being spent that way now. I cannot lay claim to the name 'composer.'" But many musicians of high rank disagree with him, and class him as a composer as well as a singer.

Mr. Burleigh has made a real contribution to the music world through his work on the music for "The Negro Spirituals." For a long time southern people thought lightly of this treasure. Many of them regarded Negro songs as a joke, and laughed over them until Negroes themselves grew half ashamed of their wonderful melodies, and for a while were reluctant about singing them in public gatherings.

But in the course of time a broader view of the unique place of Negro music in the world of art has developed. Mr. Burleigh's contribution to this cause, of such value to America and the world, has been the setting of the old melodies to a musical accompaniment so that they may be sung anywhere, by any singer, just as other songs are sung.

One of Burleigh's finest pieces of work, according to musical critics, is "Ethiopia Saluting the Colors," a setting of Walt Whitman's poem. But Burleigh has done all of his work well. "Each composition," says a musical authority, "is a classic in itself." Perhaps the most famous of this well-known group of songs is "Deep River," but it is hard to select where all are of merit. Another noted song is the setting of Rupert Brooke's sonnet, "The Soldier." "Jean" has been sung by thousands of people here and abroad, and also the "Young Warrior," a wonderful setting of a war song written by a Negro, James Weldon Johnson. This song was sung all over America and Europe by our troops during the World War.

It swept Italy like a flash. Italian soldiers sang it on the battlefield, and their people sang it at home. One musical critic has said that it is "one of the few really admirable songs America has produced in recent years."

Another one of Burleigh's great compositions is the music for a song, "Little Mother of Mine," by Walter Brown. John McCormack sang this song with wonderful effect in the New York Hippodrome before one of the largest audiences ever seen in America's largest playhouse. It is said that there were a thousand people sitting on the stage behind the singer for want of room in the main seating space. At the close of the song the audience rose in an ovation and Mr. McCormack insisted that Burleigh, who sat near him, should go forward with him to acknowledge the applause.

There is to be found also in his works the "Southland Sketches," four compositions for the violin, orchestrations for some of the songs arranged as choruses, and the "Five Songs of Laurence Hope," all of which have won high praise, and are counted among his best works.

Aside from his work as a singer and composer, Burleigh is musical editor for the American branch of the Ricardi house. No piece of music is submitted to them which does not pass through his hands, and its fate rests on his judgment.

In commenting on Burleigh, Kramer calls him "a composer by divine right." Concerning this, his publisher has also a word to say.

"He has done remarkable things," said he, "things which would have been remarkable in a man who began with everything in his favor and had no such fight to make as Burleigh had. But he has so much more in him. If only someone had had the vision, in Burleigh's youth, to set him free from that long struggle for mere existence and make it possible for him to spend his strength in the work he was made for, he would rank with MacDowell himself. One must have time for symphonies—months and years; and they bring in no ready money. America, and the whole world of art is the poorer because Burleigh had to fight for his daily bread so long."

But Burleigh himself only smiles at this. "I had my living to make," he says, "I am like other people, I must do the best I can with what I have and not cry for what I can't get."

With all of his success and achievements Harry Burleigh is modest, unassuming, and simple in his daily life.

HARRY T. BURLEIGH

1. What contribution has Mr. Burleigh made to American music?
2. Why is it said "America and the whole world of art

HARRY T. BURLEIGH

is the poorer because Burleigh had to fight for his daily bread so long?"

3. Why do some people attach such great importance to the Negro Spirituals? Why are some people inclined to laugh at them? Which is right?

4. What is the importance of the Negro Spirituals in American music?

5. What other distinct American contributions are being made to American music?

6. How do these compare with the contributions made by Negroes?

7. If Negro music were discouraged by white people would it live or die? Why?

8. How can Negro musicians be encouraged to develop further the contribution contained in Negro music?

9. What attitude should white people be encouraged to take in regard to Negro music?

10. How can America safeguard for herself and her music the talent in Negro boys and girls which corresponds to that demonstrated by Harry Burleigh?

GEORGE WASHINGTON CARVER

GEORGE WASHINGTON CARVER

GEORGE WASHINGTON CARVER was born about sixty years ago of slave parents on the Missouri farm of Moses Carver (whose name, after the fashion of slaves, the mother of the son bore). Carver's earliest recollections were the death of his father and the stealing of himself and his mother by a band of raiders in the last year of the Civil War. Moses Carver, whom George W. Carver remembers as his kindly master, sent a rescuing party on horseback liberally provided with funds to buy their release, but when the searchers overtook the marauders in Arkansas, Mary Carver, the mother, had disappeared and was never again heard from. Little George was found grievously ill with whooping cough. A race horse valued at $300 was given in exchange for him and he was returned to the Missouri farm where he was reared by his master.

Like Booker T. Washington, Carver became the rich possessor of one book, an old blue-backed speller. This he soon learned by heart, as he mastered his letters; but opportunity did not seek him out. He was forced to accept the limitations of the spelling book until he was ten years old, at which time he found his way to a Negro school eight miles away. Lodging in the cabins of friendly Negroes, sleeping in open fields or in a hospitable stable, he continued his studies for a year, keeping ever close to the soil. After graduating from this school, he set out toward Kansas, "the home of the free." A mule team overtook him a day's journey out and took him into Fort Scott where his definite schooling was begun. For nine years he worked as a domestic servant, studying day and night as his employment permitted. He specialized in laundry work and when he next moved forward he was able by the careful management and utmost frugality to complete a high-school course at Minneapolis, Kan.

After graduating from high school, Carver entered Iowa State College. Along with his studies here much of his time was given over to the management of a laundry out of which he earned enough money to meet his school expenses. Completing the work for his Bachelor's and Master's degrees, he was graduated and made a member of the faculty in charge of the greenhouse, the bacteriological laboratory, and the department of systematic botany.

Two years later Carver was discovered by Booker T. Washington who called him to his life work at Tuskegee Institute, Tuskegee, Ala. Tuskegee is now Carver's academic home, but his fame has gone throughout the nation and even into foreign countries. Thomas Edison offered this "brother wizard" a lucrative salary to join him for five years in his laboratory at Orange, N. J., and he has been made a member of the Royal Society of Arts in London, England. Carver was not even tempted to join Mr. Edison and today he does not know who proposed him for membership in the Royal Society in London. Another writer commenting on this says, "One must not suppose that Dr. Carver lacks gratitude for the honor that was implied in Mr. Edison's offer. He humbly tells one he is unworthy of it, and he is still mystified over the honor of his Fellowship in the Royal Society of Great Britain, a distinction enjoyed by a very small number of Americans."

A few years ago while the South was panic-stricken as a small black insect ravaged its cotton crops and threatened the wealth of the whole South with the "boll-weevil plague," Carver gritted his teeth and in his Tuskegee laboratory began silently to measure test tube with test tube, and then when failing crops were driving Southern planters in wholesale migrations from their farms, Carver, the scientist, stepped to the door of his workshop and pointed the South to a new source of wealth.

"The Three P's," said George Washington Carver, "potatoes, peanuts, and pecans, will form the new wealth of Dixie when cotton fails." And while men were still questioning his meaning, he brought out of his laboratory the results of patient experimentation— one hundred commercial products from the ordinary sweet potato, one hundred and forty-five from the peanut, and more than ninety-five from the pecan. His investigations had also disclosed a number of paints and colors of commercial values from the rich clay soils of Georgia and Alabama. A Negro scientist had shown the way to a new wealth for the South.

Sweet potato flour alone, which he taught the country to provide when the four million soldiers of America and the other millions of our Allies required all or most of the wheat for their sustenance, was a contribution of the utmost importance.

When the Ways and Means Committee of the House of Representatives in Washington was considering the imposition of a tariff on peanuts, among the speakers, each of whom had ten minutes of congressmen's precious time, was George W. Carver. He remained in the background until all of the white men had spoken; then he carefully measured out his statement to the bored committeemen, keeping strictly within his allotted ten minutes. But when his time was up he was not allowed to stop. Unanimously they urged him to go on. "More! More! More!" they cried.

When he sat down he had talked an hour and three quarters, in which time he told the committee of Congress of the one hundred and forty-five products which he had already discovered and extracted from the peanut, also of those he had discovered and produced from the pecan and the potato. Among the most important of these products were milk, an assortment of cheeses, caramels, chocolate bars, breakfast food, flour, instant coffee, lard, linoleum, seventeen kinds of wood stains, dye for cloth, axle grease, soap, face powder, and ink.

Referring to the many different colors which Carver has produced from southern clay, one writer says, "The magic colors which adorn the works of art in Tut-Ankh-Amen's tomb and stand resplendent and unfaded after thirty centuries, an art lost to modern workers in pigments, this magician (Carver) has reproduced in cold-water paints compounded from the clay he has dug out of the hills and pits of the South."

In 1923, Carver was awarded the Spingarn Medal which is given every year under the direction of the National Association for the Advancement of Colored People to the Negro who makes the greatest contribution to the advancement of his race.

When one asks Dr. Carver, "Are these colors which you have produced really permanent?"—"Why should they not be?" he demands in all humility, "God made the clays in the hills, they have been there for centuries with colors unchanged. All I do is to compound what God has made for man's use and delight. It is the handiwork of God—not mine. Has not the poet of the scriptures sung, 'I will lift up mine eyes unto the hills from whence cometh my help. My help cometh from the Lord who made heaven and earth and all that in them is.'"

When asked the direct question, to tell to what he attributes his astonishing success in his inventive field, Carver abandoned for a moment the attitude of the pedagogue, the manner of the laboratory investigator, and looking his questioner straight in the eye, answered succinctly, "To my God." When asked his definition of science, the reply was immediate. "They say that science is classified knowledge. I know that science is *truth*. Jesus said, 'Ye shall know the Truth and the Truth shall make you free.' It seems to me that He meant *you shall* know *Science* and *Science* shall make you free!"

No man would venture to dispute the verity of that statement who heard the soft-voiced humble disciple, Carver, declare it. Here is a man who commands the stormy seas of doubt, the billowy conflict between winds of doctrine and currents of materialistic thought, to be still—and in his presence calm must ensue. In Carver's thought, science and religion go hand and hand: back of all scientific manifestations and phenomena is the one great Cause and Creator of it all. Whether molecule or atom, back of them is life, harmony, law, God.

During the past few years leading daily papers and magazines have devoted space to the accomplishments of Carver, the great scientist and inventor. But amid this publicity and the offers which have come to him, he turns his back upon the proffered limelight and in his still small laboratory with modest equipment, he continues to work in the solitude of Tuskegee, alone with his inventive genius and "his God."

GEORGE WASHINGTON CARVER

1. What were some of the obstacles Carver had to overcome in getting his education?
2. How do the efforts Carver made to educate himself compare with the efforts of "self-made" white men?
3. To what extent do Negro boys with similar capacities

to those which Carver had deserve an equal opportunity with white boys for development along all lines?

4. How can America discover and save for herself and the world capacities such as Carver had?

5. How can white boys and girls help Negro boys and girls to have an equal opportunity in society?

6. What was the attitude of Jesus toward other races?

7. How far can we, as individuals, practice the teachings of Jesus in our efforts to help the white race afford Negroes equal opportunities?

8. Upon the basis of the above discussion, what can we do as a group now and in the future to help change unsatisfactory conditions?

DANIEL HALE WILLIAMS

DANIEL HALE WILLIAMS

WHILE the United States was seeing with dread approaching war clouds on the sore subject of abolition, Daniel Hale Williams was growing into adolescent boyhood in the small town of Janesville, Wis. Born in Hollidaysburg, Pa., in 1858, his ears must often have heard articulated hopes and prayers of his parents, Daniel and Sarah (Price) Williams, which most small boys hear before they have stopped playing with tops and marbles.

He went to high school and college in Janesville, and when only twenty years of age, he began a medical career which is outstanding.

His teacher was Gen. Henry Palmer, who had been one of the most distinguished surgeons in Illinois and Wisconsin. During the Civil War, General Palmer served on the staff of Gen. Ulysses S. Grant.

Doctor Williams left the office of his friend for work in the medical school of Northwestern University, from which he received his M.D. degree in 1883. Immediately he became a licensed practitioner in Illinois. He began to practice in Chicago and continued to labor there until 1920.

The influence of his friend, General Palmer, began to be felt there in 1884. Doctor Williams took up active surgical work under the general auspices of the South Side Dispensary. One year later he was appointed assistant physician of the Protestant Orphanage. About the same time he began the work of demonstrator in anatomy at the Northwestern Medical School from which he had graduated but two years before. The young physician held this position until 1888. Not long after this date, Doctor Williams learned that young Negro doctors and nurses were not allowed to enter the hospitals and training schools of Chicago for professional training and interneship. Feeling that this was a case for America at large, he agitated the public to such an extent that in 1892 the first training school for colored nurses was established in connection with the Provident Hospital. Doctor Williams was appointed to the post of attending physician in this hospital and for twenty years he remained at that post.

Only a year after the founding of Provident Hospital, Doctor Williams performed the first successful operation on the human heart ever recorded.

In the same year he was appointed Surgeon in Chief of the Freedman's Hospital, Washington, D. C. With his characteristic attitude toward young Negro men and girls interested in the medical profession, and again showing his ability as organizer, he thoroughly overhauled and reorganized Freedman's Hospital, setting up the Nursing School which has since become nationally famous, and putting the whole institution upon a sound professional basis.

DANIEL HALE WILLIAMS 55

This work occupied the gifted surgeon until 1898, when, at the age of forty, he married Miss Alice D. Johnson.

In 1900 Doctor Williams held the first surgical clinic,[1] of Meharry Medical College, in Nashville, Tenn. He has been professor of clinical surgery in that institution from that time until now, a record of twenty-seven years.

The Cook County Hospital of Chicago secured Doctor Williams' assistance as attending physician in 1903. For six years, despite the pressure of his many labors, the physician faithfully gave of his time in this capacity. In the same year that he gave up this work as too pressing, he received the honorary degree of LL.D. from Wilberforce University. Many have been the honors conferred upon Doctor Williams during his practice in the state of Illinois. Aside from the noteworthy positions within hospitals which have been mentioned, he has been a member of the State Board of Health (1887-1891). During the World War he served on the Board of Appeals and is now a medical examiner for the state of Illinois. He is also on the Associate Staff of St. Luke's Hospital in Chicago; is a member of the American Medical Association; of the Chicago Medical Association; and is also a fellow of the American College of Surgeons.

In the midst of his busy life, Doctor Williams has found time to write several articles on surgery which have appeared in various leading medical journals.

[1] Held for a short period yearly.

These articles have been much sought and read by physicians and surgeons throughout the entire country.

The story of this remarkable man, directly responsible for at least two outstanding nursing schools and for developing and stabilizing a clinic in one medical school, is indeed worthy of note. In fact, the contributions which outstanding Negro doctors are making to the medical profession deserve the highest praise when it is remembered that only a very few of the larger medical schools of the country admit Negroes for interne work. Through Doctor Williams' endeavors, young Negro medical students and nurses have been inspired and in a measure provided with an opportunity to complete their training as internes in standard hospitals, out of which they have come and have rendered efficient service in their various fields.

DANIEL HALE WILLIAMS

1. What would you say was Dr. Williams' greatest contribution to the Negro race?
2. Why is it true that Negro internes and nurses are not allowed to enroll for training in most of our larger hospitals?
   - a. What effect does this have upon Negro men and women who want to become doctors and nurses?
   - b. What would the evidence now available tend to prove about the ability of Negroes to become successful doctors and nurses?
   - c. Should or should not Negroes be barred from the

same training now available to white internes and nurses?

3. How can the handicaps which Negro doctors and nurses face in getting their training be lessened?

4. How can groups like ours help to increase the opportunities whereby Negro doctors and nurses may be trained?

DeHART HUBBARD

DeHart Hubbard

THE story of Hubbard's success is a story of ambition deliberately setting out to make itself fulfilled, making every needed sacrifice and letting no hardship stand in the way.

DeHart Hubbard was born in Cincinnati, in 1903. When six years of age he entered the Douglas public school and when ten he tried his first track meet. Although a seventy-five-pounder, he entered the ninety-five-pound class. He was beaten. He came back and was beaten again. "It was two years," he says, "before I won my first victory. That was a long time to wait,—but it was worth it!" After that first win he kept on winning and was graduated from Douglass school a champion in his class. He set a public school record of seven seconds for the sixty-yard dash, and had even considered jumping.

In the fall of 1917 he entered the Walnut Hills high school where he learned something of all branches of track and field sport. Before the year ended he was the school's best broad jumper with a mark of seventeen feet seven inches, and in his second year entered his first high school meet at the University of Cincinnati interscholastic games. He didn't even have any spiked shoes for the races but he did so well in the morning tryouts that some friendly "grad" let him have a pair of spiked shoes for the afternoon finals: and he became the sensation of the meet, winning the one hundred-yard dash in ten and four-fifths seconds, the broad jump at twenty feet six inches, and the hop, step, and jump at forty-three feet. It was then that he made up his mind that he was going to break the world's broad jump record and he set his heart upon that goal.

In the summer of 1922 he entered the junior national championships at Newark, N. J., and beat both "Ned" Gourdin and "Sol" Butler in the broad jump with a mark of twenty-four feet three and one-half inches.

Hubbard entered the University of Michigan for his college work and became the "iron man" of the track team. He competed in the dashes, high hurdles, and broad jump, and took every form of subsidiary training and apparatus work that would increase his broad-jumping proficiency.

When the Olympic trials came off in this country he made good and went to France as America's premier broad jumper.

The scene of the story now changes to another continent and grows picturesque: Paris, the capital of continental Europe—a huge stadium, crowded with sport followers from all sections of the globe—the 1924 Olympic Games in full swing—around the broad-jump pit a babel of tongues as clamoring fans of all nationalities urged on their favorites.

DeHart Hubbard

With America's fortunes hanging in the balance in that broad-jump contest, two American college athletes, both sons of a "sunnier clime," dug sharpened spikes into the soil of France and prepared to "do their stuff." All of America's hopes for success in that event were centered in these two colored boys—"Ned" Gourdin of Harvard University, world's broad-jump record holder and one of the great track and field athletes of all times, and DeHart Hubbard of the University of Michigan who was destined to usurp the broad-jump title.

The final jumps had started. A Norwegian—Hansen they called him—was leading with Gourdin second and Hubbard fighting his way up from a poor start. A bruised heel, the kind of injury that ordinarily makes a broad jumper tell his pit "good-bye," made each leap miserable torture for Hubbard: but with each jump he bettered his position until the time came for his fifth leap—but let him tell it.

"I knew that my fifth jump must be my last because I knew that with that racking pain in my heel I could not stand any more. I determined to put everything I had into it and I knew that I could make it. Just before the last desperate sprint down that long straightaway, I seemed to see all America gazing upon me expecting me to win, all of my race looking at me to make good, and all of my family praying for my victory. I made myself forget that sore heel and threw every ounce of energy that I could dig up into that last jump. I hit down that runway with all the speed

I could muster. Gone was caution—I took my chances on fouling the take-off. I left the ground, felt myself sailing on out through space, got in a good 'kick' and landed perfectly . . .

"A few minutes later the band was playing 'The Star Spangled Banner'—the American flag went slowly up the pole, flying high over that stadium in France above the flags of all the other nations—and there on the poles that denoted first-place and second-place victories it floated triumphantly. And down there on the field, surrounded by all nationalities of Europe, stood Gourdin and I, realizing that two colored men had carried America's colors to victory. Maybe I wasn't happy that night!"

Returning to America, Hubbard kept up his training and on June 13, 1925, at Stagg Field, Chicago, Ill., he broke the world's broad-jump record with a leap of twenty-five feet ten and seven-eighths inches.

What normal, husky, red-blooded man would not have been happy? What normal boy would not be willing to go through that same intense training, that same unyielding perseverance that carried DeHart Hubbard to an Olympic victory and later to a world's championship?

Running through that simple story of Hubbard's supreme effort, like a refrain, are the keynotes expressed in the chance phrases of Hubbard himself:—"America expecting me to win," "My race looking at me to make good," "My family praying for my victory." "And I made myself forget," he said, "and threw every ounce of energy I could muster into that last jump."

If no story of Hubbard's earlier years were told, if no record of patient, laborious practice hours, of taking defeats only to come back a victor were related, in those four catch phrases would be summed up his whole secret of success. For when all is said and done, the incentives that bring out the most there is in any man, be he athlete, soldier, or poet, are the urge of country, the urge of race, the urge of family—and, backed by these, the determination to forget all else but the goal to be attained. "I threw every ounce of energy I could muster into that last jump," he said. Certainly no man has a right to be satisfied with his success until that "last ounce" of energy is summoned, and he finds himself doing just a little bit "better than he knows how!"

But Hubbard's success started on the public school playgrounds, at the age of ten, in the races he lost to scrapping rivals. He stuck to the job and learned to beat them and that knowledge and that habit carried him to a world's championship.

Aside from broad jumping Hubbard has also made records in the fifty-, sixty-, sixty-five-, and one hundred-yard dashes. Below are his records for 1925-1926.

1925

100 yards	9⅗ seconds	(Record)
50 yards	5⅕ seconds	(Record)
60 yards	6⅕ seconds	(Record)
Broad jump 25 feet 10⅞ inches		(Record)

IN SPITE OF HANDICAPS

1926

100 yards	9⅗ seconds (Record)
65 yards	6⅘ seconds (Record)
Broad jump	25 feet 2½ inches (A.A.U. record)

Hubbard has won the broad jump for the fifth consecutive time in the A.A.U. championships and is now devoting his time to public recreation in the city of Cincinnati, Ohio, teaching the boys of his home town how to grow physically strong. He has turned his back on several flattering offers from professionals to commercialize his athletic prowess, and content himself in serving the boys of his community.

DeHART HUBBARD

1. How and at what age did Hubbard's athletic career begin?
2. What seem to be the incentives and principles of training that underlie his success as an athlete?
    a. What was Hubbard's attitude toward commercialized athletics?
3. How do Hubbard's career and athletic achievements compare with those of the athletes of other races and nations? Should America honor him as it does Paddock? Why or why not?
4. What honors has Hubbard won for America through his athletic ability?
5. Why do some of our larger American universities bar Negro student athletes from certain major sports?
6. To what extent should Negro students be given an equal opportunity with white students to participate in all

forms of athletics in schools and colleges where both races attend?

7. How can our public schools and colleges discover and train for themselves and America other athletes with such possibilities as Hubbard had?

8. How can our schools and athletic directors help athletes to develop such high ideals that they will train to excel as athletes rather than for commercial purposes when they leave school?

9. What lessons can we get from Hubbard's career that will help us excel in life?

10. How can we, as individuals, and as a group help other boys to develop high ideals in our sports?

11. What should be our attitudes toward athletes of different races?

WILLIAM EDWARD BURGHARDT DuBOIS

WILLIAM EDWARD BURGHARDT DuBOIS

DOCTOR DuBOIS divides his life into four periods: "The Age of Miracles, The Days of Disillusion, The Discipline of Work and Play, and The Second Miracle Age." In following closely his career, one can easily see the reason for these sharp divisions.

William Edward Burghardt DuBois was born at Great Barrington, Mass., Feb. 23, 1868, the son of Alfred and Mary DuBois. Poverty cast its shadow over his boyhood during which time a new suit was an event and the provision of the household necessities caused more than one anxious moment to his mother. His education was begun in the public schools of Great Barrington where he was graduated from the high school.

The "Age of Miracles" began when, at the age of seventeen, he received a scholarship granting him four years of study in Fisk University, Nashville, Tenn. After completing the work at Fisk for the A.B. degree, life unfolded new miracles at Harvard. Money, scholarships, fellowships, another Bachelor's and a Master's degree came to him. Then, through the Slater Fund came financial aid which enabled him to study two years in Germany. In 1895 he presented his thesis, "The Suppression of the Slave Trade," and received from Harvard his Ph.D. degree. Dr. DuBois calls this period of scholastic attainment an age of miracles but the fact must not be overlooked that all of these advantages came to him because of his persistent effort and ability to excel in his school work.

The dark, dreary "Days of Disillusion" came just after DuBois had completed his work for the Ph.D. degree, when he went to Wilberforce University to teach Greek and Latin for a salary of $750 a year. He remained there living within the narrow world of this small college hampered by the dead sphere of the Greek and Latin languages until the scene changed to Philadelphia where he made his study of the Negro life of that city for the University of Pennsylvania.

The period of the "Discipline of Work and Play" began at Atlanta University where for thirteen years he taught sociology and planned for the future, working out his dream of a great organization with a powerful organ to fight the battles of his people. While in Atlanta, "The Atlanta University Studies" were done and the "Souls of Black Folk" was also completed.

Dr. DuBois' doctor's thesis became the very first volume in the Harvard historical series. His writings are listed in the Harvard University Library as promptly as they are given to the publishers; among his writings, in addition to his Harvard thesis, are his study of the Philadelphia Negro, and probably the most notable of his works, the collection of essays

WILLIAM EDWARD BURGHARDT DuBOIS

which comprise "The Souls of Black Folk." His biography of John Brown was published in 1909; the "Quest of the Silver Fleece" appeared in 1911; his one-volume history, "The Negro," came out in 1915. In 1920 he published another collection of essays under the title, "Darkwater," and in 1924, "The Gift of Black Folk" was published.

The "Second Miracle Age" began when Dr. DuBois entered the conflict which was precipitated by the challenge of a younger generation of intellectuals to the ascendency of Booker T. Washington and the school of thought which had grown up around him. Quickly aligning himself with the opponents of the Washington faction, he found himself at the head of a great wing of new thought (which was then called radical). Out of this school of thought the Niagara Movement was born and the sentiment created expressed itself finally in the organization of the National Association for the Advancement of Colored People.

This Association was organized to combat what DuBois and his associates considered a dangerous school of thought and to champion the cause of the Negro for justice and advancement along all lines of social, political, and educational endeavor. It has since become one of the most effective propaganda organizations maintained by any racial group in America. The present membership exceeds one hundred thousand and is composed of both colored and white Americans. The official organ of the Association is *The Crisis,* of which Dr. DuBois is the editor. *The Crisis* was first issued in July, 1910, and is as truly the production of its editor as the Association is an expression of his dream. Through the National Association for the Advancement of Colored People, which in a large measure has been built up around Dr. DuBois, he is working steadily, and with sure strokes, to bring about that larger recognition of the equality of all real manhood which he had dreamed of one day helping to establish.

As a lecturer, Dr. DuBois has entrée to the platform of the foremost American universities and he has been elected a fellow of the American Association for the Advancement of Science. The Pan-African Congress, a production of DuBois' dream of a union of the darker races throughout the world, was founded by him: and he has already seen it assembled in three biennial conventions in the capitals of Europe.

Few men, armed as DuBois was armed for conquest in a dozen fields, have been able deliberately to turn their backs upon the world's measure of success that might have been theirs, for a life's service to what at times seemed all but a "lost cause." As a writer with a style of intense, fragile beauty; as a lecturer of broad experience and scholarly attainment; as a public figure whose contacts would have won him desirable berths, he might have selected a career that would have led far to the rewards most men demand of life. But as a dreamer with an unswerving determination to make his dreams come true, Dr. DuBois has given to his nation an outstanding example of idealism in an age of pragmatism, and to his race an effective organization to champion their cause of which he dreamed long before it was given him to work out.

A scholar of the Old World and of the New, steeped in the lore of the University of Berlin and of Harvard, yet contented still to devote his broad, deep intellect to the interpretation of "The Souls of Black Folk," and to their cause for educational, social and political freedom, William Edward Burghardt DuBois—editor, author, lecturer, and publicist—occupies today a place unique in the life of the Negro race and of America.

WILLIAM EDWARD BURGHARDT DuBOIS

1. On what does DuBois base his belief that Negroes ought to enjoy all the privileges of American life which white people enjoy?
   a. To what extent are these claims just?
   b. Does DuBois ask any privileges or opportunities for Negroes that the white race does not have or already enjoy?
2. What caused DuBois to be called a radical?
3. What importance do you attach to *The Crisis*[1] in moulding public opinion?
   a. To what extent is *The Crisis* read by white people? Why?
   b. To what extent do the masses of Negroes read *The Crisis?* Why?

[1] The official organ of the National Association for the Advancement of Colored People, edited by DuBois.

c. What class of people among the two races read *The Crisis* most? Why?

4. Would you say that DuBois is or is not investing his exceptional talents to the best advantage? Why?

5. What good would it do for all colored and white people who believe as Dr. DuBois believes to join the National Association for the Advancement of Colored People and subscribe to *The Crisis?*

6. How can interested white and colored people help on this issue between the races?

JOHN HOPE

JOHN HOPE

FOR a long time the supporters of higher education for Negroes, and the public in general held the belief that the presidency of schools of collegiate standing for Negroes must be filled by white men. In fact, most Negro colleges, until recent years, were presided over by white men, mostly ministers carrying out the missionary point of view. This popular conviction did not begin to change until a few colored men were given a chance to demonstrate their ability as college executives.

One of our first and most successful college presidents is Dr. John Hope. When Dr. Hope became president of Morehouse College it was, like most colleges in the South for Negroes at that time, a college merely in name. Very little progress had been made in standardizing the course of study and the faculty was composed almost entirely of men without advanced degrees.

During Dr. Hope's administration the college faculty has been strengthened, the physical equipment improved and enlarged, the course of study standardized, and the college has received recognition by our leading universities. Because of the demonstration of efficiency which Dr. Hope has made as a college president, much of the doubt which was formerly in the minds of the public as to the ability of colored men to administer successfully the affairs of schools of collegiate standing has been removed, and the way has been opened for an increasing number of Negroes to become college presidents. Dr. Hope's admirable example is being followed by such men as President John W. Davis of West Virginia Collegiate Institute, and Dr. Mordecai W. Johnson of Howard University, and, by the way, both of these men are graduates of Morehouse College, having studied under Dr. Hope's administration.

John Hope was born in Augusta, Ga., June 2, 1868, the son of James and Mary Frances Butts Hope. He has been self-supporting since the age of eleven. Without the least help he has fought his way across a "no-man's land" of obstacles to a position where Brown University, his Alma Mater, was glad to elect him in 1919 to honorary membership in Phi Beta Kappa, "for achievement since graduation," while other universities have given him honorary degrees.

Two months after his conversion, declares Hope, a Baptist minister led him in the way to his life work. "I was then eighteen years of age," he writes, "and I at once quit my job and went to school. I had been out of school five years but I went to Worcester Academy and registered. I intended to be a minister of the gospel but later I came to doubt that my own spirituality was sufficient for the task."

After graduation from Worcester Academy in June,

1890, he entered Brown University in Providence, R. I., and worked his way through the four years of college study.

"While floundering about," he writes, "I hit upon the idea of teaching. The idea came to me suddenly one day in my junior year as I was pondering over the choice of a vocation. At once I talked the matter over with my roommate. Then I went to see the president of the University and had a talk with him. Both advised my taking up teaching. Since my graduation from college, I have put into that work every ounce of energy that I possess." Yet in a footnote with which many boys will sympathize, he whimsically confesses: "My chief difficulty, I am afraid, has been laziness. My friends, indeed, might almost call it a disease!" But John Hope proved to be his own doctor. He prescribed for the disease and conquered it.

From 1894 to 1898 he was at Roger Williams College in Nashville, Tenn. While teaching there he married Miss Lugenia D. Burns of Chicago, Ill., Dec. 29, 1897. In the year 1898 he was called as a professor to Morehouse College (then known as Atlanta Baptist College). In 1906 he became the president of this institution.

The doctrine of service by which he has let his own life be guided at Morehouse is illustrated in a letter of congratulation to a Y M C A official. "May I welcome you most cordially," he wrote, "into your new field and wish you the highest success, as this success is to come to you in a better, nobler boyhood throughout America as far as our Y M C A can reach this boyhood."

Dr. Hope holds an M.A. degree (honorary, 1907) from Brown University; an LL.D. (honorary) from Bucknell, 1923; and from Howard, 1920. "He is now a director and trustee of several institutions for advancement work with his race and is constantly active," says "Who's Who," "in the amelioration of conditions among Negroes in the South."

The Atlanta Neighborhood Union stands as a monument to John Hope and his wife and their aim of service. The social settlement house was started by the ladies of the college, led by Mrs. Hope, to reach the needy of Atlanta. Today it is a center of social service activities.

Dr. Hope has done more than preach to boys and young men the doctrine of service: he has lived out his teaching. When the call to arms sounded through the nation in the early days of 1917, John Hope, ever true to his doctrine of life, left his work at Morehouse College for what he deemed a more urgent service at that time. For twelve months, from July, 1918, to July, 1919, he labored in France alongside pupils who were fighting in the combat divisions, as a Y M C A worker. Dr. Hope is a member of the National Council of the Y M C A and is also a member of the World's Committee of the Y M C A.

Service to his race in the three decades since his graduation from college, to his country in the two years of its warring on European soil, and to his God in that upbuilding of clean youth to which his life is dedicated, has marked the brilliant career of John Hope, president of Morehouse College, and one of the most distinguished graduates of one of New England's oldest colleges.

JOHN HOPE

1. In what aspect of Negro attainment has John Hope been an outstanding pioneer?
2. Why was it believed that Negroes were not able to lead in the administration of Negro institutions of higher learning?
3. What obstacles did Dr. Hope have to overcome to accomplish his goal?
4. What significance has his accomplishment been:
    a. To the Negro race?
    b. To the white race?
    c. What difference does it make to Negro boys that they can now receive in the South the same advantages open to white boys in colleges and universities under the direction of their own race?
    d. If Negro boys were limited to institutions for industrial education only how serious would the result be?
5. How can Negro boys take advantage of the educational facilities which Dr. Hope has helped to open up for them?
6. How can groups of white boys and girls help in spreading the movement of higher education for Negroes of which Dr. Hope is a pioneer?

ARCHIE ALPHONSO ALEXANDER

ARCHIE ALPHONSO ALEXANDER

AMONG the men of the Negro race who are graduates of northern universities and who have made good in highly specialized vocations or business, A. A. Alexander is perhaps one of the most successful and yet one of whom the public has heard but little. Mr. Alexander is a civil engineer and general contractor with offices at 505 Frankel Building, Des Moines, Ia. The fact that Mr. Alexander is not very widely known may be attributed to the following reasons: First, he is overly modest and shuns publicity and notoriety whenever possible. Second, his only business associate, George F. Higbee, now deceased, was a member of the white race. Third, because of the very nature of his business, it has been transacted almost entirely with white business men. Therefore, his contacts with colored men who would seek to give publicity to his work have been limited.

Mr. Alexander is purely an Iowa product. He was born in Ottumwa, Ia., May 14, 1888. He attended the public schools of Des Moines where he was graduated from the high school in 1905. After staying out of school for a while, he entered the College of Engineering in the University of Iowa, from which he was graduated in 1912 with the Bachelor of Engineering degree.

Being an older son in the large family of a humble laboring man, Alexander was compelled to work and earn his own way through high school and college. But fortunately for him, he was blessed with a magnificent physique and a good mind which enabled him to withstand hard work, keep up his studies and find time for athletics. His scholastic standard was high and he made such an enviable record on the varsity football teams of 1909, 1910, and 1911, that he was dubbed by the university students "Alexander the Great," by which name he is still known on the university campus.

After graduating from the university, he was employed for two years as designing engineer for the Marsh Bridge Company of Des Moines. While in the employment of this company, he formed the acquaintance and gained the friendship of George F. Higbee who was similarly employed and with whom he formed a partnership in 1914. They entered into the business of general contracting under the firm name of Alexander and Higbee, specializing in the designing and the construction of concrete and steel bridges. Their partnership continued up to the date of the accidental death of Mr. Higbee which occurred in the spring of 1925 as the result of his having been struck by a steel beam while supervising the erection of a bridge. Since that time Mr. Alexander has continued the business alone. Though feeling greatly the loss of his partner, his business has gone forward with increasing success.

During the winter of 1921, Mr. Alexander went to England to take a post-graduate course in bridge designing in the University of London. In June of 1921 he was recalled to his Alma Mater and the honorary degree of Civil Engineer was conferred upon him. He was further honored by the University of Iowa when it awarded him the contract of constructing a concrete conduit about a mile in length connecting the university heating plant with the original campus.

Among the other outstanding engineering jobs which he has designed and constructed are the Forest Avenue viaduct in Des Moines, the South Des Moines sewer system covering a stretch of thirty-seven miles, the widening and repaving of the Sixth Avenue bridge in Des Moines, and the construction of the Coon River siphon, all of which contracts were secured from the city council through regular bids.

Other notable structures designed and erected by Mr. Alexander are the James River viaduct at Mitchell, S. D., Skunk River bridge at Grinnell, Ia., and the River bridge at Mt. Pleasant, Ia., which is said to be the largest highway bridge ever constructed in the state.

It is conservatively estimated that since 1914 Mr. Alexander has done a yearly business of about a half million dollars. At the present writing he has under contract two large construction jobs—one a seven-span concrete viaduct for Iowa City; the other a combined heat, light, power, and water plant for the University of Iowa costing approximately $500,000.

Mr. Alexander's phenomenal success as a civil engineer tends to discredit the general belief by many people that there is no opportunity or future for the Negro in this and similar specialized vocations. The fact is that none of these specialized vocations will be open to the Negro unless he prepares himself to enter them as Mr. Alexander has done. His preparation was thorough and the efficiency with which he does his work enables him to surmount many of the difficulties incurred by racial boundaries and to secure large contracts through the process of regular bidding with white competitors.

Notwithstanding the fact that his business relations have been chiefly with members of the white race, Mr. Alexander is an ardent supporter of all worthwhile movements for the betterment of his own race. He is a charter member of the first executive committee of the Des Moines Branch of the National Association for the Advancement of Colored People. It should also be said that he is the founder of the Omega Chapter of the Kappa Alpha Psi Fraternity and is chairman of the board of directors. He has been a continuous member of the committee of management of the Crocker Street Branch Y M C A since its organization in 1919. In 1925 Mr. Alexander was awarded the "Laurel Wreath" given by his fraternity, Kappa Alpha Psi, annually to the member of the fraternity who has accomplished the most outstanding thing during the year. This award was presented to him at the Grand Chapter meeting in Washington in December, 1926.

In addition to this, he was awarded a bronze medal and $100 in cash by the Harmon Foundation for being the second most outstanding Negro in the business world during the year 1926. This award was presented by Honorable Fred H. Hunter, Mayor of Des Moines at the Des Moines Lincoln-Douglas Day celebration on Feb. 14, 1927.

In 1913 Mr. Alexander was happily married to Miss Audra Linsay of Denver, Colo. To them there has been born one son, "A. A., Junior." Their residence, an elegantly finished bungalow, is also the product of Mr. Alexander's own designing and construction and is reputed to be one of the best homes in the city of Des Moines.

Mr. Alexander is a man of but few words. He believes in doing instead of talking. He says that when he was a lad he read that Abraham Lincoln said that if one will only prepare himself for his life's work, his opportunity will come some day, and that this has been the guiding principle of his life. Unquestionably, he has made good under it.

ARCHIE ALPHONSO ALEXANDER

1. With what life callings are Negroes most closely associated in the public mind? Why is this?
2. In what callings do we find Negroes making a place for themselves on a par with the most successful white leaders?
3. Are such Negroes to be explained as exceptions in their ability, or as having had advantages superior to their

84 IN SPITE OF HANDICAPS

Negro brothers?. Why do you believe as you do? How do you explain Mr. Alexander's calling and success?

4. What evidence is there that the abilities of Negroes are limited to fewer callings than the abilities of white or yellow races?

5. What evidence is there that the capacities and abilities of the Negro race are as unlimited as those of the white or yellow races?

6. If the belief that Negroes are not as capable as other races were proven to be prejudice and not based on scientific fact what would such evidence mean to the Negro race? To the white race?

7. The evidence of science does go to show that the Negro race is handicapped by its environment and not its capacity. Science would show Mr. Alexander's ability, calling, and success to be the expected thing of the Negro race rather than the exception. Why are such facts not generally known?

8. How can groups such as this help to overcome prejudices by scientific facts?

MATTHEW W. BULLOCK

MATTHEW W. BULLOCK

FOR a long time the opinion was held that the field of law offered little or no opportunities for Negroes to rise to places of distinction. In fact, there was a tendency on the part of some white people to discourage Negroes from pursuing law, for fear that the study of law would awaken political interests in them and at the same time equip them with power to fight for political rights.

Among the best trained and most successful lawyers of the Negro race at the present time is found Matthew W. Bullock of Boston, Mass. Attorney Bullock was born Sept. 11, 1881, in Dabney, N. C.

Fortunately for Matthew, his parents, Jesse and Amanda (Sneed) Bullock, though they had served in slavery, were eager that their children should receive an education. Finding themselves with their little family located in an environment where educational advantages for Negroes were well nigh impossible, they moved to Boston, Mass., where the children could attend school.

Matthew was eight years of age when his parents left North Carolina. He attended the public schools of Boston for five years and then entered the public schools of Everett, Mass., where he was graduated from the high school in 1900.

As well as being an honor student, he was a lover of outdoor sports. During his senior year at the Everett high school he was elected captain of the hockey, baseball, and football teams. These were recognitions or honors given only to a few and the best athletes of "E. H. S."

In the fall of 1900, Bullock entered Dartmouth College and soon became prominent in the life of the school. It was soon discovered that he had a good voice and he was elected to membership in the Glee Club, which he held for four years.

For scholastic achievement he was made a member of the honorary senior society (Paleopitus) and was also a member of several other exclusive boards, committees, and student societies.

It was also at Dartmouth that he became nationally known as a football star. For three years he was a veteran on the varsity football team and helped to win many victories of which Dartmouth will always be proud. Not only is Matthew Bullock's name familiar to the students and grads of Dartmouth, but it is a fond memory in the minds of many old football fans throughout the country.

He was also held in esteem as a track man, having been a member of the track team for the four years of his stay at Dartmouth. Upon his graduation from Dartmouth, in 1904, with the B.A. degree, he entered the law school of Harvard University from which he was graduated in 1907 with the LL.B. degree.

It is of more than passing interest to note that after Bullock had prepared himself so well for success in the practice of law in 1907, he did not begin regular practice until 1921, but he gave these fourteen years of his life to service which could hardly be measured in dollars and cents. With his interests still high in athletics, he sought out a position as football coach for the Walden, Mass., high school which he held for two years. He was called from this position to the Massachusetts Agricultural College as football coach, where he served for three years. In 1908 he accepted a position as teacher and director of athletics at Morehouse College in Atlanta, Ga.

Bullock remained at Morehouse for four years, during which time he produced some of the fastest and cleanest football squads in the South.

While in Atlanta he married Miss Katherine H. Wright, in 1910. To them two children have been born, Matthew W., Jr., and Julia Amanda.

Bullock gave up his position at Morehouse College in 1912 and practiced law in the city of Atlanta for two years, after which he was called to the Alabama Agricultural and Mechanical School as dean of the college. He served admirably in this position for two years, at the close of which, in 1917, he became Y M C A Educational Secretary at Camp Meade, Md. After serving in this capacity for three months he went to France with the Three Hundred Sixty-ninth U. S.

Infantry (Fifteenth New York Regiment) and served as Y M C A War Work Physical Director with the troops for fifteen months.

Upon his return to the States in 1919 he became executive secretary of the Boston Urban League and served in this position for two years.

In 1921 he gave up his work with the Urban League and took up the practice of law in the city of Boston, where he has continued in this profession with increasing success until the present time.

With his wonderful background of training and experience he has put into his profession an unusually high humanitarian idealism, which has won for him the esteem and admiration not only of the citizenry at large but of his colaborers in the legal profession as well.

For the four years of 1921 to 1924, inclusive, his duties as a practicing attorney were performed with such diligence, honesty, and efficiency, that, in 1925, he was appointed Special Assistant Attorney General for the state of Massachusetts, in which position he is serving at the present time. He is also a member of the State Board of Parole.

Attorney Bullock is demonstrating in his practice that a lawyer does not necessarily have to cater to the whims of petty politicians or play into the hands of the "boss" in order to achieve distinction and success in his profession.

Aside from the heavy duties that devolve upon him as a lawyer, he finds time to become active in civic and social life. He is a member of the Knights of Pythias,

MATTHEW W. BULLOCK

the Masonic Order and the Omega Psi Phi college fraternity.

In all of his professional and civic duties, honesty and efficiency have been the guiding principles in his life, and he attributes his success to the part that these have played in his every endeavor.

MATTHEW W. BULLOCK

1. In how many athletic teams in high school and college did Bullock win recognition?
2. On what basis would you suppose he was selected as coach in a State School when the student body was 95 per cent white?
    a. What would some people say about the appointment of a colored man as coach in a white school?
    b. On what basis would some defend it?
    c. Would you say that Bullock was or was not capable of holding the job as coach? What evidence do you have to support your view?
    d. Should the election of a coach be based on ability or color? Why?
3. What evidence is there that Bullock was versatile in his capabilities?
4. Would you say he was or was not a successful lawyer? Why?
    a. What attitude is taken by some people in regard to Negroes entering law?
    b. What causes such attitudes?
    c. What importance should be attached to such attitudes?

5. Should or should not Negroes who desire to practice law be encouraged to do so? Why?

6. What attitudes should be taken toward Negroes entering politics?

7. Should government officials be selected on the basis of ability or color? Why?

8. What can groups like ours do to open up opportunities in the professions of law and politics for Negroes?

HENRY OSSAWA TANNER

HENRY OSSAWA TANNER

HENRY OSSAWA TANNER was born in the city of Pittsburgh, Pa., June 21, 1859, the son of Bishop Benjamin Tucker Tanner and Sarah Elizabeth Miller. He studied at the Pennsylvania Academy of Fine Arts under Thomas Eakins, and nothing more was needed to convince him of what had been his earliest conviction—that he was born to paint. From the beginning, he wanted to be an artist. His life seems to place him in that large class of exemplifiers of the rule that "if you want a thing hard enough, you'll get it."

When Tanner was quite young his father moved to Philadelphia, in order that the lad might be nearer his study, and he stayed with Eakins for four or five years. He studied drawing, modelling, and painting. No side of his field was neglected, and even today the making of portrait busts remains for him a favorite method of artistic expression. In his early days he produced a bust of Bishop Daniel Payne.

But painting was Tanner's forte, and he worked faithfully on landscapes, marines and anything that might give him self-expression in the field that he so passionately loved. It was love for his work that kept him at it, for there was little financial reward.

One of his early paintings, he reminisces, was after no little difficulty sold for $15 to a dealer who later resold it for $250. His genius could not forever go unrecognized, and a sketch done in Atlantic City—"A Windy Day on the Meadows"—brought him $100. The picture now hangs in the Academy of Fine Arts.

This gave him the needed encouragement, and in the last month of 1891 he gathered what small savings he had accumulated, and with nothing more than a faith in his ability to make good and an irresistible determination to make the grade, he sailed for Europe. He became a pupil of two masters, Benjamin Constant and Jean-Paul Laurens, who conducted a studio together, and gained from this alliance the rare benefit of contrasted moods and techniques, from which it is probable that he evolved his own—a third—style. M. Constant, one of the master artists of the Paris of that day, became Tanner's mentor and friend; he gave of his best efforts to the young student.

Paris immediately claimed Tanner. He made several trips back to the United States, but always the call of France was heeded, and Paris repaid his devotion. He gained entrée to the Salon exhibits, and in 1897 his "Raising of Lazarus" won the gold medal and was purchased by the French government. With surer hand and truer eye he continued at this task and year by year he rose nearer that mark he had set for himself.

In 1889, the "Annunciation" which now hangs in Memorial Hall, Fairmount Park, Philadelphia, Pa., was made a part of the Wilstack collection. Two years later "Nicodemus Coming to Christ" was purchased by the Pennsylvania Academy of Fine Arts for its own galleries. The Lippincott prize came to him, and the field of religious painting beckoned him to enter not as a novice but as a master whom the world of art was now glad to recognize.

In 1898, he married in London a Miss Jessie Macauley and the couple started their life in Paris. Their son, Jesse, is now studying at Cambridge University in England.

Today art lovers from all nations look to Tanner's newest paintings. Like all of the truly great, he limits his output; three pictures a year are his goal. His paintings are for that reason even the more vied for, for the homes of men like Andrew Carnegie, for the galleries of Pittsburgh, and the museums of Boston, New York, and Chicago.

Prizes of every sort have been lavished upon his work. His "Two Disciples at the Tomb" won the Harris award, and in 1907 the French government honored him and bought his "Disciples at Emmaus" for the Luxemburg where the finest of Europe's treasures hang.

With all his honors and his interest in art, Tanner found time to help the American government in the World War, as a Red Cross worker, getting as near the front as Neufchâteau, in charge of convalescent camps.

Among his paintings which have attracted the most attention in American galleries are "The Holy Family," "Mary and Elizabeth," "Christ Walking on the Sea,"

"Christ Learning to Ride," "Hills Near Jerusalem," "The Hiding of Moses," "A Lady of Jerusalem," and "Christ at the Home of Lazarus."

Among his medals and awards have been the Salon honorable mention in 1896, the third-class medal in 1897, the second-class medal in 1907, the Walter Lippincott prize in Philadelphia in 1900, the Harris prize in Chicago, the second medal in the Paris exposition of 1900, the second medal in the Buffalo exposition of 1901, the second medal at the St. Louis exposition of 1904, the gold medal at the San Francisco exposition of 1915.

He has exhibited in the Luxemburg, the Wilstack collection, Carnegie Institute, Academy of Fine Arts, Philadelphia, Chicago Art Institute, the Los Angeles Art Gallery, and the Des Moines Art Gallery. He is a Knight of the Legion of Honor, and an Associate National Academician, as well as a member of the Paris Society of American Painters and of the American Art Association.

HENRY OSSAWA TANNER

1. What are some of the obstacles which Tanner encountered in achieving his success?
2. How do Tanner's achievements compare with other artists (white and colored) who have followed a similar line of painting?
3. Should Tanner be recognized and treated by society upon the basis of his racial identity or should he be recognized and treated as an artist? Why?

4. To what extent do boys of all races here in America, with similar capacities to those which Tanner had, deserve an equal opportunity for development along all lines? Are there exceptions?

5. How can America provide an equal opportunity for all boys irrespective of race?

6. What steps can we take to discover and develop our own capacities?

7. How can we help other boys and girls discover and develop their capacities?

JAMES WELDON JOHNSON

JAMES WELDON JOHNSON

THE career of James Weldon Johnson offers a striking study of an accomplished, versatile man of affairs. He is a poet at heart. Aside from this field he demonstrated a soundness of business judgment and the shrewdness of political calculation that kept him for seven and a half years in Uncle Sam's consular service. As a servant of the National Association for the Advancement of Colored People, he has focused his many-sided talent upon the work of securing justice and an equal opportunity for Negroes in America to whom justice is often denied. In each of his callings Johnson has shown an astonishing capacity for reaching the topmost rungs of the ladder of success.

James Weldon Johnson was born in Jacksonville, Fla., June 17, 1871, the son of James and Helen Louise Dillette Johnson. His education was begun in the schools of Jacksonville. Later he entered Atlanta University from which he was graduated in 1894 with the A.B. degree, and was given the Master's degree in 1904. He also did three years of graduate work at Columbia University in New York. In 1917 he received an honorary degree of Litt.D. from Talladega College, Talladega, Ala.

After serving for several years as principal of the

colored high school in Jacksonville, Fla., Johnson moved to New York to collaborate with his brother (J. Rosamond Johnson) in writing for the light-opera stage. Songs written in collaboration with his brother were sung by leading artists and comparatively few people who enjoyed the grand opera "Goyescas" presented at the Metropolitan Opera House in New York City during the season of 1915 realized that the libretto was written from the original by a Negro, James Weldon Johnson.

As a poet, Mr. Johnson is turned to by leading literary magazines where an authoritative criticism of the poetry of the race is sought. A review of the Negro Spirituals and folksongs by Johnson is but lately off the press. His "Book of American Negro Poetry" is a standard volume, while his contributions in verse to *The Crisis, The Century,* and *The Independent* have been collected and published in a volume called "Fifty Years and Other Poems." Of his poem, "Fifty Years," commemorating the fiftieth anniversary of the Emancipation Proclamation, no less a man of letters than Brander Matthews wrote, "It is one of the noblest commemoration poems yet written by an American . . . a poem which any living poet might be proud to call his own."

In 1906, Johnson was appointed United States consul to Puerto Cabello, Venezuela. After serving in this position for three years he was given the position of consul to Corinto, Nicaragua, in which position he also served admirably for three years.

Mr. Johnson is now executive secretary of the National Association for the Advancement of Colored People. As an officer of this organization he has traveled from coast to coast, lecturing, doing organization work, and enlisting the support of hundreds of fair-minded people whose admiration has been compelled by his scholarly addresses. Under his leadership the branch work of the Association has been more thoroughly organized and the influence of the Association has been made effective in high places, the most notable among which was the famous Sweet case which was fought and won by the Association in Detroit in 1925. Mr. Johnson possesses a rare gift for presenting effectively, with succinct force, the merits of his cause in a manner to compel response from men placed high in authority.

Aside from the honor of his position in the National Association for the Advancement of Colored People, he is a member of the Board of Directors of the American Fund for Public Service, a member of the American Academy of Political Science, a member of the American Ethical Society, and a member of the New York Civic Club.

Poet, consul, attorney, lecturer, and composer of theatrical books, James Weldon Johnson, present executive secretary of the National Association for the Advancement of Colored People and generally heralded as a leading spirit in the field of Negro poetry, represents perhaps in a fuller measure than any other single individual of his generation the great versatility of his race.

JAMES WELDON JOHNSON

1. List some of the reasons why Dr. DuBois and Dr. Johnson feel that the National Association for the Advancement of Colored People is necessary.
2. Should the work of this Association be encouraged or discouraged? Why?
    a. Why do some Negroes refuse to work with it?
    b. Why do some white people believe it should be discouraged?
    c. Why do many Negroes belong to and work through it?
    d. Why do many white people belong to and work through it?
    e. Why do men of such great talent as Dr. Johnson and Dr. DuBois consecrate their lives to this Association?
3. Of all the viewpoints about this Association which seem to you to be based on prejudice? Why? Which seem to be based on social customs which ought to be changed? Which seem to be based upon the truth?
4. What viewpoint would the teachings and principles of Jesus point to as being right?
5. What can groups like this do to overcome the prejudices which the National Association for the Advancement of Colored People is striving to eradicate?
6. How can white people be helped to practice respect for the rights and attainments of Negroes?
7. How can colored people be helped to a greater belief in their own abilities?
8. How can colored people increasingly demonstrate their

ability and alertness to take advantage of all the opportunities enjoyed by white people in America?

9. To what extent do the lives of men like James Weldon Johnson help?

MARY McLEOD BETHUNE

MARY McLEOD BETHUNE

THE most outstanding traits in the character of Mary McLeod Bethune are a superb courage which makes her immune from fear or despair, an intense interest in others, a yearning to help them, and a strong, simple, abiding faith in her Heavenly Father—the kind of faith which verily removes mountains of difficulty from her path of unselfish service.

Mrs. Bethune was one of a family of seventeen children. She was born of slave parents, Sam and Patsy McLeod, in a humble cabin on a rice and cotton farm near Mayesville, S. C.

Early in life, she began to show little distinctive traits of character. Her little tasks were always performed swiftly, neatly and cheerfully. Her devotion to her parents and her desire to help them in every possible way, her quick understanding sympathy made her their "comfort and joy."

When Mary was about eleven years old, a little school was opened near Mayesville by the Board of Missions of the Presbyterian Church, and Mary was one among the first children who walked the four miles to school and back. Her mother said, "We had to make some of the children go, but it seems like Mary, little as she was, kinda understood what it all meant. She was that happy to go and was the first one out on the road with her little bucket on her arm anxious to get started."

In a few years the little school had done its best for Mary, and Miss Emma Wilson, her beloved teacher, told her one day that Miss Mary Crissman, a dressmaker in Denver, Colo., wanted to pay for a little girl to go to school to Scotia Seminary, and that she, Miss Wilson, had chosen Mary to go, because she had done so well in school.

With a heart overflowing with joy, the child ran home with the good news, and in the autumn she bade good-bye to the old friends, the old scenes, and a pitiful, lonely little girl with a song in her heart took her first railroad journey to Scotia Seminary. She was awkward and shy enough at first, but she met every slight, every criticism with unfailing good humor, and soon won the hearts of teachers and students alike.

At the close of her work at Scotia Seminary she received a scholarship which enabled her to continue her studies at the Moody Bible Institute in Chicago. Life seemed rapidly unfolding for Mary, and she found great delight in her work at the Institute.

At the end of her term (two years) at Moody Institute, Mary hoped to see the fulfilment of a long cherished hope to go to Africa as a missionary, but bitter disappointment awaited her. At the Presbyterian Board of Missions, she learned that all of the colored stations in Africa were filled; and she was appointed as a teacher at Haines Institute, Augusta, Ga., of which school Miss Lucy Laney was principal. One who knew her in those days said: "It was a delight to note the real enthusiasm with which Miss McLeod entered into her first work." In a short time, with the true missionary spirit, she had gathered a large group of little children from the streets and was holding with them a most inspiring and helpful "Mission School" on Sunday afternoons. Mrs. Bethune often speaks of the joy of that service and the inspiration that she imbibed from that rare spirit, Lucy Laney.

The next post to which our earnest worker was sent was to Sumter, S. C., where she taught for two years, then she was married to Albert Bethune, a teacher, and moved to Savannah, Ga. Two years were spent in quiet home life. During this period her only son, Albert McLeod Bethune, was born. Then, again came a call to public service—this time to Palatka, Fla.

At this point, she taught the Mission School and rendered a most remarkable service—visiting, singing, and reading to the prisoners in the county jail. Many thrilling stories are told of her influence for good upon the lives of many of the prisoners and the help that she sometimes gave in freeing those who were unjustly accused.

As necessary and encouraging as this work was, there still seemed to be an urge to move on, and the end of five years found her on her way to Daytona, with her little boy.

After paying her fare, she had $1.50 in her purse,

but there is no way of estimating the value of her faith, her courage, her yearning to serve her people and her God.

Arriving at Daytona, she found that, though a perfect stranger there, the Master had one of His servants waiting to help her. A good woman gave her food and shelter, and went with her the next morning in search of a house in which to open the school which she felt impelled to establish for Negro girls.

The house being found, there was no furniture, but with characteristic resourcefulness, the earnest woman procured dry-goods boxes from stores, and bits of discarded matting or carpet, a bed or two, and proceeded to make or repair furniture as the case demanded. At last the little cabin was in readiness, and on the fourth day of October, 1904, in a room where everything was very simple—crude even, but scrupulously clean—Mrs. Bethune stepped to the door, her eyes shining, her heart aglow, and rang the little bell which a friend in Palatka had given her. Five little girls responded, and the Daytona Educational and Industrial Training School (so she named it then) was founded, with the repetition of the Twenty-third Psalm, the singing of the old hymn—"Leaning on the Everlasting Arms"—and a fervent prayer for help and guidance.

Trials and struggles have accompanied the growth of the institution under the guidance of Mrs. Bethune. But with true Christian faith, hard work and fair play, this lone woman has succeeded in the thing she started out to do. The little cabin is replaced by a beautiful campus, thirty-two acres of land, fourteen buildings—a plant estimated conservatively at $600,000. The confidence of the public has been secured and kept. For twenty-two years the school has been supported by public contribution, and every improvement—every new building, every addition in equipment or teaching staff—has been the outcome of prayer and toil on the part of Mary McLeod Bethune.

In 1923, the Daytona Normal and Industrial Institute was merged with Cookman Institute, of Jacksonville, Fla., and became coeducational. It was then placed under the auspices of the Board of Education of the Methodist Episcopal Church. Its founder and guiding spirit, however, is still active in making the institution, now known as Bethune-Cookman College, more fitted to meet the needs of Negro youth in this section.

Mrs. Bethune was the leading spirit in establishing a Home for Delinquent Colored Girls at Ocala, Fla. She has served as president of the Southeastern Federation of Women's Clubs, and in 1924, at Chicago, was unanimously elected as president of the National Association of Colored Women—the leading organization of colored women in the world. At Oakland, Calif., in August, 1926, she was reelected to this position, and today she represents 200,000 of the most cultured and consecrated women of the race. She has served as president of the National Association of Teachers in Colored schools, and is now an active member in the

Interracial Council of America. Perhaps no woman of her race has given herself more unselfishly and fearlessly toward securing the highest good for her people. The school which she founded has had a phenomenal growth. From five little girls it has developed to a Junior College with an enrollment of over four hundred students, with a plant equipment comparing favorably with other colleges of like grade. "Their training," she writes, "is of the head, hand, and heart, and in them the principles of Christian citizenship are instilled."

MARY McLEOD BETHUNE

1. What Negro schools and colleges do you know of?
2. How do they compare with neighboring white schools and colleges?
3. On the whole do Negro boys and girls have a poorer or equal or a better chance for education than do white boys and girls? What evidence have you which bears out your belief?
    a. Why was Mrs. Bethune interested in establishing her school in Daytona?
4. How do you account for the attitude which the different states and sections of the country take toward the education of Negroes?
5. What provisions, if any, does the Constitution of the United States make in this regard? Does it discriminate on the basis of color? Why? How do state and local governments handle this question?
6. What do the principles and teachings of Jesus suggest in regard to inequalities and injustices?

7. How can the educational opportunities and facilities for Negro education be bettered?

8. How can America help to establish other institutions such as the Bethune-Cookman College?

9. How should America treat Negro educators such as Mrs. Bethune?

10. How can groups such as this help in the betterment of opportunities for Negro education?

MAX YERGAN

MAX YERGAN

NOT too many years ago a bright-eyed boy sat at his aged grandfather's side. The grandfather was bent with years of toil which he had spent in slavery. There was a close resemblance between grandson and grandparent along the line of general features.

"My days are nearly spent," said the grandfather, "but it is my hope that some day a grandson of mine will go as a missionary to our people in Africa."

The small boy, Max Yergan, was born in Raleigh, N. C., in 1892. Deep in his heart this wish of the old man must have persisted unnoticed, for he says, "It may have been the subconscious factor in my final decision to become a missionary. At any rate it comes to me now as a priceless memory."

It was in the fall of 1911 that Max Yergan first came to the attention of Y M C A leaders. William A. Hunton, David D. Jones, and C. H. Tobias, then student secretaries of the International Committee of the Y M C A, were conducting a Bible Study Institute at Shaw University, Raleigh, N. C. They noticed among the young men of the committee of arrangements, a particularly bright fellow scarcely out of his teens who busied himself in making the visiting delegates welcome and in cooperating with the leaders in the carrying out of the program.

The following spring this same young man accompanied the Shaw delegation to the Kings Mountain Student Conference. At the conference, he showed the same spirit of willingness to help by assisting the leaders in booking student interviews and doing almost everything that came to hand in helping to make the conference function smoothly and effectively. After this first conference session, he became one of the officials of the Shaw Y M C A and was sent to the student conference annually.

In 1914, the Kings Mountain Conference was not held because of the holding of a great student convention in Atlanta. Yergan was not a delegate from Shaw to this convention but so strongly had he impressed himself upon one of the student secretaries that this secretary made it possible for him to attend the convention by lending him the money to pay his expenses. It was at this convention that Yergan made his final life-work decision. Previous to this time, he had been thinking of studying law. At the Sunday afternoon meeting of the convention, which was composed of nearly a thousand delegates—students and faculty members from eighty different institutions—he was on the program for brief remarks along with three other young men, and in his remarks he stated that when he came to that convention he was thinking of the profession of law as a life work but that the messages of the convention and the whole atmosphere had so influenced him that he had come to the decision of devoting his life to some form of Christian service. This was his senior year at college.

The following year, after having made up his mind that he would do Y M C A work, he went to Springfield Training College. After studying there a year he was called into the service of the International Committee to work among the students of the Southwestern field.

At the close of his first year of service in this field, he attended the International Convention of the Y M C A at Cleveland. While there he heard, among other messages, a ringing appeal from E. C. Carter, then National Secretary of the Y M C A work in India. This was in 1916, just in the midst of the World War. Carter was making an appeal for forty men to go back with him to India to serve the native troops. This appeal so strongly impressed Yergan that he came immediately from the convention to the Student Conference at Kings Mountain and made known to Dr. J. E. Moorland, then Senior Secretary of the Colored Work Department, and to C. H. Tobias, who was directing the Student Conference, that he had heard this appeal of Carter's and had decided that he should respond to the appeal. Both Moorland and Tobias told him that they did not see how they could do without him, so critical was the situation in the student field at that time, with Tobias, upon whom the major responsibility rested for directing the work, in a precarious condition of health, but that if it seemed to be the clear call of God that he should go to India they would not stand in the way.

This was in June. Within five weeks of this time he was on shipboard with more than thirty other men on their way to India. He served several months in India and then was told that he had the opportunity of going into either the Mesopotamian or East African campaigns accompanying the Indian troops. He found difficulty in choosing between these two fronts. How he had longed to go to Mesopotamia where he might see those Bible lands about which he had heard from his early boyhood! The call of the blood was stronger, however, and he decided in favor of going to East Africa. Accompanying a detachment of Indian troops he landed in the late fall of 1916 at Dar-Es-Salaam, East Africa. There he remained for nearly two years serving all kinds of troops—Indian, West Indian, and troops from all parts of Africa.

In spite of repeated attacks of African fever, he did his work so well that Major Webster, the British official in charge of the Y M C A work in the area, cabled to Dr. John R. Mott in America that if he had any other colored young men like Yergan to send six others to East Africa. Dr. Mott read this cablegram to the colored members of the National Staff assembled at Atlantic City and requested that they get busy immediately to find six additional men. Beginning at Atlantic City with a young man who was rolling chairs on the boardwalk, a form of summer work that Yergan himself at one time engaged in, the six young men were recruited and sent to Africa.

Yergan was privileged to remain several months after they arrived but at the end of his two-year period, he was so weakened by fever that he had to be invalided home. It was while he was lying in his hammock on the deck of the vessel just before it sailed that he heard the screams of the African boy who had looked upon him as friend and older brother for several months, that the need of permanent Association work among the natives was indelibly impressed upon him. As he sailed out of the port of Dar-Es-Salaam with the shrieks of this boy echoing and reechoing in his mind and heart, he determined that he would return to Africa.

Upon reaching America, an attempt was made to have him divorce everything from his mind and take a much needed rest. This he refused to do, insisting that he had to go into the schools and colleges to make known to the students what he had seen in Africa and to challenge them to a response in gifts of money and life in the interest of Africa's redemption. He set out upon his journeys with a weakened body but a determined heart.

After several weeks of this sort of visitation he was called into the service of the United States Army—the United States then being in the World War. He was made a chaplain and stationed at Camp Lee, Va., where he served until the close of the war and the mustering out of the troops.

Following his discharge from the army, it became necessary for the Y M C A War Work Council to send him to France to finish up work among the colored units of the Expeditionary Army. This being completed, he returned to America and started upon the agitation which resulted in the action of the International Committee in authorizing the initiation of work among the natives in Africa.

Yergan was chosen as the first worker and sailed for South Africa in November, 1921. Upon arrival at Cape Town, he encountered suspicion on the part of government officials and even on the part of church workers, for American Negroes are always viewed with suspicion in South Africa until they prove themselves and the worthwhileness of their mission, as Yergan finally did.

In his five years of labor among the natives of South Africa, he organized twenty-six Associations among the students and initiated interracial discussion groups in the colonial colleges and universities which have led to better understanding between the Colonials and the natives. So far-reaching has been his work that he is now looked upon as one of the Christian statesmen of that part of the world.

At the High Leigh Conference of the World's Student Christian Federation, 1924, he was elected one of seven members of the Executive Committee of that organization, thus showing the confidence the leaders of the student movements of the world have in his leadership.

South Africa, the field in which Yergan is working,

presents one of the most difficult racial situations on earth. Five million Africans have been suddenly brought into contact with modern civilization. Their labor and cooperation are sought by the million and a half white residents of that country. These Africans are centuries behind the world's advance. When they take residence in the cities they are wholly unprepared for the many temptations which they face. The scale of living is much higher than that of the simple village life to which they have been accustomed. Schools for Africans have been established by missions and are now considered by the government. In the schools young men and women become aware of the great progress of the world and of the difficult road ahead of their own people to find a place in modern life.

Yergan's task is to hearten these young people, to carry to them a message of hope, to show them how to relate their learning to their own neighboring tribes and to give to them a brighter outlook upon life and the world about them. He visits all the schools which fall within his area. To do this he must traverse the almost treeless expanse of South Africa for three thousand miles. He is in effect a "circuit rider of the veldt."

It is hard for us, living in the United States, to measure what Max Yergan stands for with the African people. Each tribe claims him as their own and he claims kin to all. He tells an interesting story of how an old man of the Xosa tribe looked him long in the face one day, and solemnly assured him that he belonged to the Xosa people. At any rate, to hear Yergan pronounce the name, beginning with a choke and ending with triumphant clearness, would convince one of his "kindship." But it is not the kinship of blood which moves him so much as the kinship of spirit. To strengthen the hearts of the students, to see the children of heathen homes gather for instruction for games and even singing marches, is his reward for long journeying and toil. During the five years in South Africa he has seen young men and women develop as leaders. He has seen enough of their applied Christian methods to feel sure that there is hope for his people.

Yergan shows a keen interest in the research which is now being made by African men to preserve to their posterity, century-old folklore and customs of the tribes, much of which will be speedily lost unless gleaned from the old men of each tribe. Letters from South Africa quote Yergan as the foremost leader of his people. Of his work in conference with the white leaders of the country and his contribution to race understanding he is too modest to speak, yet various reports bring to us accounts of the inestimable service which he renders in this connection. Indeed modesty is one of the most engaging qualities of this cultured man whom any race would be proud to claim.

In December, 1926, he was awarded the Harmon Prize for the greatest contribution made during the year to the religious life of the Negro race.

Yergan has spent several months during 1926-1927 in America on furlough, visiting schools and colleges

MAX YERGAN

both white and colored throughout the country in the interest of his work in South Africa and the Y M C A movement throughout the world. He will return to South Africa in the fall of 1927 to resume the work in which his whole life and thoughts have been wrapped up.

He is still a young man but all will agree, who take the time to look over his record, that his early manhood years have been crowded with service to his fellowmen.

MAX YERGAN

1. Make a list of the varieties of things which Yergan has done in his thirty-five years of life.

2. Which of these prove most conclusively that Yergan has a sense of mission and self-confidence?

3. How does the average American boy compare with Max Yergan in this sense of mission and self-confidence?

4. How important to a worthwhile life is this sense of mission—self-confidence?

5. How does a boy go about the development of this self-confidence and mission in life?

    a. What in Yergan's early manhood and college days contributed to this sense of self-confidence?

6. Of what importance to this sense of self-confidence is the habit of service to others?

7. Of what importance to this sense of mission is the habit of good workmanship?

8. How can boys of today develop such habits?

9. Yergan seemed constantly to be looking for chances to help some one else. How can boys of today develop such a habit?

CARTER G. WOODSON

CARTER G. WOODSON

WHEN inquiring minds seek authentic information concerning the Negro race, they turn quickly to the works of Dr. Carter G. Woodson, author, editor, and publisher of historic data concerning Negro life.

Dean Kelly Miller has given a very succinct yet comprehensive statement concerning Dr. Woodson's work in which he says:

The social importance of history, or perhaps, I had better say, the importance of social history has become but recently appreciated. As a schoolboy, I used to read in the textbooks that history was a record of the deeds and doings of important personages and people. Distinguished achievements and spectacular performances monopolized the entire field of recorded human action. The ordinary deeds and doings of ordinary people did not rise to the level of the historian's concern. But in more recent times we are beginning to recognize that any performance, individual or *en masse*, which influences the course of human progress or retrogression is deemed a contributory factor of history. If no single slave ever rose above the benumbing drudgery of hewing wood and drawing water, nevertheless, slavery and the slave could not be omitted from any trustworthy account of the civilization of the South, and indeed, of the nation. Dr. Woodson has somewhere made a sharp distinction between the history of the Negro and the Negro in history. Too often the artist makes the mountain peaks suffice for the whole landscape. The infinitely smaller eminences and depressions are apt to be ignored by the painter bent on exploiting dominant features. But not so with the scientific historian. The battle may be lost for the want of the horseshoe nail as well as for lack of the imperious general. It is said that the loss of the Battle of Waterloo, which turned the tide of European history, might have been attributed to the careless cook whose beefsteak affected Napolean's usual alertness and enabled the Duke of Wellington to take advantage of his momentary dullness. Henson, the black attendant, accompanied Peary to the North Pole. The menial part played by this sable attendant was an important and essential part in polar discovery. Dr. Woodson is concerned in digging out every significant rôle which the Negro has played in the world's drama. This makes our history, not only full and complete, but true to the actualities of historic happenings.

Dr. Woodson was born of ex-slave parents near New Canton, Buckingham County, Va., Dec. 19, 1875. His father was John Henry Woodson, and his mother, Anne Eliza (Riddle) Woodson. As he was one of a rather large family, his parents, who started life in poverty, could not provide him with the ordinary comforts of life and could not regularly send him to the five-month district school after he was old enough to work on the farm. In this rural school, however, he managed largely by self-instruction to master the fundamentals of common school subjects by the time he was seventeen. At this age, in 1892, he went with his brother

Robert Henry Woodson to West Virginia, to which his parents were induced to move the following year, settling at Huntington. Young Woodson, however, had to accept employment in the coal fields in Fayette County, where he labored as a miner for six years, spending a few months annually in school.

In 1895 he entered the Douglass High School of Huntington, W. Va., the course of which he completed in less than two years, receiving a diploma there in 1896. He then entered Berea College in Kentucky, famous at that time because of its coeducation of the races. There he studied a part of two years and then began teaching, starting first at Winona, Fayette County, W. Va., in 1898. From Winona, he was called to the principalship of the Douglass High School, of Huntington, from which he had been graduated four years before. He then spent his summers studying at the University of Chicago, where he finally obtained the degree of Bachelor of Arts.

He traveled and studied a year in Asia and Europe, spending one semester at La Sorbonne, the University of Paris, under the instruction of Professors Aulard, Diehl, Lemonnier, and Bouche-Leclerc. There, he not only did graduate work in history, but in having contact with French as it is spoken, he learned to speak the language as fluently as he had already learned abroad to speak Spanish.

Returning to the United States, he resumed his studies at the University of Chicago, from which he received the degree of Master of Arts in 1908. After studying a little further at Chicago, he went to Harvard to continue his research work in history and political science, specializing under Professors Charles Gross, Ephraim Emerson, W. B. Munro and Edward Channing. In 1909 he accepted a position as instructor in romance languages in the Washington high schools that he might make the necessary research in the Library of Congress to write his doctoral dissertation, "The Disruption of Virginia," which was accepted at Harvard in 1912, when he received the degree of Doctor of Philosophy.

Dr. Woodson served in the Washington public school system ten years, offering instruction in French, Spanish, English, and history. The last two years of this service was in the capacity of instructor in English and the history of education at the Myrtilla Miner Normal School and principal of Armstrong Manual Training High School. From 1920 to 1922 he served as dean at the West Virginia Collegiate Institute, reorganizing the College Department. At the expiration of this service, Dr. Woodson retired altogether from teaching to devote all of his time to research in connection with the Association for the Study of Negro Life and History.

This Association was organized by Dr. Woodson in Chicago on Sept. 9, 1915, with five persons, namely, Dr. George C. Hall, Alexander Jackson, J. E. Stamps, W. B. Hartgrove, and the founder. It was incorporated under the laws of the District of Columbia on the third of the following October. The purpose of this undertaking is to preserve and publish the records of the Negro in order that the race may not become a negligible factor in the thought of the world. The Association has endeavored to collect sociological and historical documents of Negro life and history to publish therefrom informing books, that the world may not forget what the race has thought and felt and attempted and accomplished.

An important purpose of the Association is the publication of *The Journal of Negro History*, a quarterly scientific review of one hundred pages of current articles and documents giving facts generally unknown. This publication has been regularly issued since January, 1916, and has reached its tenth volume. In bound form it constitutes a veritable encyclopedia of information concerning the history of the life of the Negro in this country and abroad. It circulates among scholars throughout the civilized world, since it appeals especially to colleges and universities of both races as a desirable aid to social workers and students carrying on research.

The Association has directed the attention of investigators to this neglected field and stimulated the study of Negro history through local clubs and classes in institutions which have done much to change the attitude of white people toward the Negro. The Association is indorsed by some of the most distinguished men in the United States and in Europe. Among these may be mentioned Harold H. Swift, Oswald Garrison Villard, Morton D. Hull, A. S. Fissell, Cleveland H.

Dodge, J. Franklin Jameson, J. R. Angell, William Renwick Riddell, Walter Weyl, and Sir Harry H. Johnston.

During these years of painstaking research, Dr. Woodson has written a number of books dealing with neglected aspects of Negro history. The first of these, "The Education of the Negro Prior to 1861," appeared in 1915, evoking from the leading organs of thought in the United States most favorable comments to the effect that it showed both original treatment and independent research. His next work was "A Century of Negro Migration," brought out in 1918 at the time of the culmination of the exodus of the Negroes to the North. In this work the author connected the recent movement of the Negroes with various other efforts which have affected the Negro population during the last hundred years.

Recently Dr. Woodson has published through the Associated Publishers two very popular works, "The History of the Negro Church," and "The Negro in Our History." The treatise on the church undertakes to present the religious development of the Negro in our panorama, sketching the coming of the early missionaries, the appearance of the Negro preachers as the result of liberalizing influences, the rise of the African church, its struggle with forces without and within, and finally its triumph as a socializing institution around which develops the new life of a rising race.

"The Negro in Our History" has proved to be the most popular of all. This is a well-illustrated textbook planned to meet the long-felt want of a suitable work for students desirous of knowing the leading facts of Negro life and history. In this work there has been treated every important phase of history influenced by the Negro. Beginning with the situation in Africa, the author discusses the enslavement of the race at home and abroad; the sort of bondage experienced; the first steps for its amelioration; the reaction against the Negro; the economic aspect of slavery, abolition, colonization; the question in Congress; the Civil War; the reconstruction; the readjustment; the achievements of the race in freedom; the Negro in the World War; and the struggle for social justice. It has been well received by the press, the school, and the pulpit as a much-needed contribution to American historical literature destined to secure for the Negro race a new hearing at the bar of public opinion. The book has now reached its third edition in a revised and enlarged form.

Dr. Woodson has recently produced three other important works, "Negro Orators and their Orations," "Free Negro Heads of Families," and "The Mind of the Negro as reflected in letters written during the crisis, 1800-1860."

Dr. Woodson has made every possible sacrifice for the cause to which he is devoted. In the beginning of the movement he beggared himself that the work might succeed. The work of the Association for the Study of Negro Life and History won the approval of the historical scholars of the country. The historical department of both Harvard and the University of

Chicago, where Dr. Woodson has studied, at once recognized the importance of what he was endeavoring to do. A few philanthropists began to find out what was being accomplished and furnished substantial assistance.

With funds obtained through these sources, the Association has been studying the free Negro prior to the Civil War and the Negro in the reconstruction of the southern states. The project has gone far beyond the ability of one man to operate. Dr. Woodson has on his staff several carefully trained Negro students in present-day historical methods through whom, under his direction, much of this research work has already been accomplished. In this effort, too, the investigation is not restricted to the Negro in the United States. The Association has an investigator working in the archives of the Indies, one in Seville, Spain; one making an investigation in the British Museum, and the Public Record Office in London; and still another in Hayti studying folklore. The Association has thereby been enabled to accomplish worthwhile work which speaks for itself.

As a recognition for his contribution to the race in 1926, Dr. Woodson was awarded the Spingarn Medal which is given by the National Association for the Advancement of Colored People to the member of the race who has made the most outstanding achievement during the year.

CARTER G. WOODSON

1. Recall the men who are described in this book. Make a list of their callings.
2. How would you characterize the contributions this group of men have made to American life?
3. In what specifics do you believe their lives will affect the history of America? Of the Negro?
4. What importance do you attach to the Association for the Study of Negro Life and History which will preserve the records of the lives of these famous Negroes?
   a. What attitude should America take toward Dr. Woodson's work?
   b. In what particulars will the work of this association be helpful to the Negro race? To the White race?
5. How can groups such as this take advantage of the work of the Association for the Study of Negro Life and History?

BIBLIOGRAPHY

Some Books By Negro Writers

Biography:
- ALEXANDER, C., "The Battles and Victories of Allen Allensworth," 1914.
- ALLEN, RICHARD, "Life," 1833.
- ANDREWS, R. M., "John Merrick, A Biographical Sketch," 1920.
- BRAWLEY, BENJAMIN, "The Negro in Literature and Art," 1910.
- BRENT, LINDA, "Linda, or Incidents in the Life of a Slave Girl," 1861.
- BROOKS, W. S., "Footprints of a Black Man in the Holy Land," 1915.
- BROWN, WILLIAM WELLS, "The Black Man," 1863.
- COPPIN, L. J., "Unwritten History, An Autobiography," 1919.
- DAVIS, D. WEBSTER, "The Life and Public Service of the Reverend William Washington Brown," 1911.
- DOUGLASS, FREDERICK, "My Bondage and Freedom," 1855; "Life and Times of Frederick Douglass," 1882.
- DUBOIS, W. E. B., "John Brown," 1909.
- EDWARDS, W. J., "Twenty-five Years in the Black Belt," 1918.

BIBLIOGRAPHY

Evans, Dr. Matilda A., "Martha Schofield, Pioneer Negro Education," 1916.

Floyd, Silas X., "Life of Charles C. Walker, D.D.," 1902.

Fuell, Melissa, "Blind Boone, His Life and Achievements," 1915.

Fuller, T. O., "Twenty Years in Public Life," 1913.

Gaudet, Mrs. Frances Joseph, "He Leadeth Me," an Autobiography, 1913.

Gibbs, M. W., "Shadows and Light," an Autobiography, 1902.

Green, J. P., "Fact Stranger than Fiction. Seventy-five Years of a Busy Life," an Autobiography, 1920.

Hare, Maud Cuney, "A Life of Norris Wright Cuney," 1913.

Haynes, Elizabeth Ross, "Unsung Heroes."

Henson, Matthew A., "A Negro at the North Pole," 1912.

Holtzclaw, W. H., "The Black Man's Burden," 1915.

Johnson, James Weldon, "The Autobiography of an Ex-colored Man," 1912.

Jones, L. C., "Piney Woods and Its Story," 1922.

Lane, Bishop Isaac, "Autobiography."

Langston, John M., "From a Virginia Plantation to the National Capital," 1894.

Moton, R. R., "Finding A Way Out," an Autobiography, 1920.

Northup, Solomon, "Twelve Years a Slave," 1853.

Pickens, William, "The Heir of Slaves," 1911.

Randolf, E. A., "Life of the Rev. John Jasper," 1884.

Simmons, W. J., "Men of Mark," ———.

Smith, Amanda, "Autobiography," 1893.

STEWARD, T. G. "Fifty Years in the Gospel Ministry," 1920.
TROTTER, J. M., "Music and Some Highly Musical People," 1885.
TRUTH, SOJOURNER, "Sojourner Truth's Narrative," 1875.
WASHINGTON, BOOKER T., "Up from Slavery," 1900; "Frederick Douglass," 1907; "My Larger Education," 1912.

Miscellaneous:
LOCKE, ALAIN, "The New Negro," 1926.

History:
ARNETT, B. W., "Proceedings of the Quarto-centenary Conference," 1865-1890, 1890.
BEASLEY, DELILAH L., "The Negro Trail Blazers of California," 1919.
BOWEN, J. W. E., "Africa and the American Negro," ——.
BRAGG, G. F., "Afro-American Church Workers," 1861; "Men of Maryland," ——; "The Episcopal Church and the Black Man," ——; "How the Black Man found the Church," ——.
BRAWLEY, B. G., "Short History of the Negro," 1913; "The Negro in Literature and in Art," 1918; "A Social History of the American Negro," 1921; "Africa and the War," 1918; "Women of Achievement," 1919; "History of Morehouse College," 1917.
BRUCE, J. E., "A Tribute for the Negro Soldier," ——.
CAMPBELL, ROBERT, "A Pilgrimage to My Mother Land," 1861.

BIBLIOGRAPHY

Coppin, L. J., "Unwritten History," 1919.
Cromwell, J. W., "The Negro in American History," 1914.
DuBois, W. E. B., "The Suppression of the Slave Trade," ———.
Hicks, W., "History of Louisiana Negro Baptists, 1804-1914," 1915.
Hood, J. W., "History of the A. M. E. Zion Church," ———.
Hunton, Addie W., and Johnson, Kathryn M., "Two Colored Women with the American Expeditionary Forces," 1920.
Majors, M. A., "Noted Negro Woman," 1893.
Mason, M. and Furr, A., "The American Negro Soldier with the Red Hand," 1920.
Moore, J. J., "History of the A. M. E. Zion Church," 1880.
Mossell, Mrs. N. F., "Afro-American Women," 1918.
Murray, Daniel, "Encyclopedia of the Negro," 1912.
Payne, Daniel A., "History of the A. M. E. Church," 1890.
Penn, I. Garland, "The Afro-American Press," ———.
Phillips, C. H., "History of the C. M. C. Church," ———.
Scott, E. J., "The American Negro in the World War," 1919.
Steward, Mrs. S. M., "Women in Medicine," 1915.
Steward, T. G., "The Haitian Revolution," 1914.
Still, William, "The Underground Railroad," 1872.
Vass, S. N., "Progress of the Negro Race," 1906.
Washington, Booker T., "The Story of the Negro," 1909.

BIBLIOGRAPHY

WILKES, LAURA E., "Missing Pages in American History, Negro Soldiers in Early Wars, 1641-1815."
WILLIAMS, C. H., "Sidelights on Negro Soldiers," 1923.
WILLIAMS, GEORGE W., "History of the Negro Race in America," 1882; "Negro Troops in the Rebellion," 1888.
WILSON, JOSEPH T., "History of the Black Phalanx," ——.
WOODSON, C. G., "The Negro in Our History," 1924.
WOODSON, C. G., "The History of the Negro Church," 1921.
WOODSON, C. G., "Negro Orators and Their Orations."
WRIGHT, R. R., JR., "Centennial Encyclopedia of the A. M. E. Church," 1916.
YOUNG, CHARLES, "Military Morale of Nations and Races," 1912.

Education:
BRADY, ST. ELMO, "Household Chemistry for Girls," ——.
BULLARD, MABLE HURT, "Heart to Heart Talks with Teachers," 1922.
CRUMMELL, ALEXANDER, "The Attitude of the American Mind Toward the Negro Intellect," 1898.
DUNBAR, ALICE M., "Masterpieces of Negro Eloquence," 1913.
GRIGGS, SUTTON E., "Life's Demands or According to Law," ——.
JONES, G. H., "Education in Theory and Practice," 1919.
LOVINGOOD, R. S., "Why Hic, Haec, Hoc, for the Negro," 1900.
PAYNE, DANIEL A., "Domestic Education," 1885.

PHILLIPS, J. T., "A Quick Review in English Grammar," 1913.
TIMBERLAKE, C. L., "Household Ethics and Industrial Training Colored Schools," 1913.
WASHINGTON, BOOKER T., "Character Building," 1903; "Working with the Hands," 1904.
WRIGHT, R. R., "Negro Education in Georgia," 1894.

Religion:
BOOTH, C. O., "Plain Theology for Plain People," ——.
BOWEN, J. W. E., "National Sermons," ——.
BOYD, R. H., "Sunday School Commentary," 1909.
BLYDEN, E. W., "Christianity, Islam, and the Negro Race," 1887.
CARTER, R. A., "Morning Meditations and Other Selections," 1917.
CRUMMELL, ALEXANDER, "The Greatness of Christ," ——.
HAMILTON, F. M., "Hand Book on Colored Methodism," ——.
HENDERSON, G. W., "Sermon Studies," 1917.
LEE, R. L., "Racial Episcopacy," 1915.
PENN, I. GARLAND, and BOWEN, J. E. W., "The United Negro, etc., Proceedings of the Negro Young People's Christian Congress," 1902.
RANKIN, J. W., "Hand Book of Missions," ——.
SHEPPARD, W. H., "Presbyterian Pioneers in the Congo," 1917.
SHORTER, SUSAN L., "Heroines of African Methodism," 1891.
TALBERT, HORACE, "The Sons of Allen," 1906.
TANNER, BENJAMIN T., "An Outline of History and Government of the A. M. E. Churchmen," 1884.

BIBLIOGRAPHY

THOMAS, I. L., "Methodism and the Negro," 1911.
WAYMAN, A. W., "My Recollections of the A. M. E. Ministers," 1883.

Poetry:

BATTLE, MRS. EFFIE T., "Gleamings from Dixie Land," 1916.
BRAITHWAITE, W. S., "Lyrics of Life and Love, etc.," ——.
BURLEIGH, LOUISE ALSTON, "Echoes from the Southland," ——.
CAMPBELL, JAMES E., "Echoes from the Cabin and Elsewhere," 1895.
CARMICHAEL, W. T., "In the Heart of a Folk," 1918.
COTTER, J. S., "Band of Gideon and Other Lyrics," 1918.
DANCER, W. E., "Today and Yistidy," 1914.
CULLEN, COUNTEE, "Color," 1925.
DAVIS, D. WEBSTER, "Weh Down Souf," 1897.
DUNBAR, PAUL LAURENCE, "Lyrics of Lowly Life," 1899; "Lyrics of the Hearthstone," etc., 1901.
FLEMING, SARAH LEE BROWN, "Clouds and Sunshine," 1920.
HAMMON, JUPITER, "Poems," 1916.
HARPER, FRANCES E. W., "Miscellaneous Poems," 1854; "Sketches of Southern Life," 1896; "Poems," 1900.
HILL, L. P., "The Wings of Oppression and Other Poems," 1921.
HOLLOWAY, J. W., "From the Desert," 1919.
HUGHES, LANGSTON, "The Weary Blues and Other Poems," ——.

JOHNSON, ADOLPHUS, "The Silver Chord," 1915.
JOHNSON, FENTON, "A Little Dreaming," 1914; "Visions of the Dusk," 1915.
JOHNSON, MRS. GEORGIA DOUGLAS, "The Heart of a Woman and Other Poems," 1918.
JOHNSON, J. W., "Fifty Years and Other Poems," 1917; "The Book of American Negro Poetry," 1922.
JONES, E. SMYTH, "The Sylvan Cabin," 1911.
JONES, J. H., "Poems of the Four Seas," 1921.
MCCLELLAN, G. M., "The Path of Dreams," 1916.
MCGIRT, JAMES E., "Some Simple Songs," 1901.
MCKAY, CLAUDE, "Songs of Jamaica," 1912; "Constab Ballads," 1912; "Spring in New Hampshire," 1921; "Harlem Shadows," 1922.
MEANS, STERLING M., "The Deserted Cabin and Other Poems," 1915.
RAY, CORDELIA, "Poems," 1910.
SCHOMBERG, ARTHUR A., "A Biographical Checklist of American Negro Poetry," 1916.
SHACKLEFORD, WILLIAM H., "Poems," 1907.
WHEATLEY, PHYLLIS, "Poems," 1835; "Poems and Letters," 1916; "Bibliography of Her Writings," 1916.
WHITMAN, A. A., "An Idyll of the South," 1901.

Fiction:

ADAMS, C., "Ethiopia, The Land of Promise," 1917.
CHESTNUTT, CHARLES W., "The Conjure Woman," 1899; "The Wife of His Youth and Other Stories," 1899; "The House Behind the Cedars," 1900;

BIBLIOGRAPHY

"The Marrow of Tradition," 1901; "The Colonel's Dream," 1905.

DuBois, W. E. B., "The Quest of the Silver Fleece," 1911.

Dunbar, Mrs. Alice Ruth Moore, "Goodness of St. Rocque and Other Stories," 1899.

Dunbar, Paul Laurence, "Folks from Dixie," 1898; "Love and Landry," 1900; "Strength of Gideon and Other Stories," 1902; "Uncalled," ———; "Heart of Happy Hollow," 1904.

Fauset, Jessie R., "There Is Confusion," 1924.

Fleming, Sarah Lee Brown, "Hope's Highway," 1917.

Fullilove, Maggie Shaw, "Who Is Responsible," 1919.

Gilmore, F. Grant, "The Problem of Military Novel," 1915.

Griggs, Sutton E., "Unfettered," 1902; "The Hindered Hand," 1905.

Grimke, Angelina W., "Rachel," a play in three acts, 1920.

Harper, Mrs. F. E. W., "Iola Leroy," 1892.

Hopkins, Pauline, "Contending Forces," ———.

Johnson, Fenton, "Tales of Darkest America," 1920.

McGirt, James E., "The Triumph of Ephriam," 1907.

Shackleford, William H., "Along the Highway," 1915.

Walker, T. H. B., "J. Johnson, or the Unknown Man," 1915.

White, Walter F., "The Fire in the Flint," 1924.

Wright, Zara, "Black and White Tangled Threads," 1920.

Music:

BURLEIGH, HARRY THACKER, "Plantation Melodies," 1901; "Two Plantation Songs," 1905; "Ethiopian Pæan," 1910; "Oh South Land," 1919; "Ethiopia Saluting the Colors"; "Deep River"; "The Soldier"; "Jean"; "Young Warrior"; "Little Mother of Mine"; and others.

COOK, WILL MARION, "Mandy Lou—In Dahomey."

DETT, R. NATHANIEL, "American Negro Music," 1918-1919.

HARE, MAUD CUNEY, "Six Creole Folk Songs with Text," 1921.

JOHNSON, JAMES WELDON, "A Book of American Negro Spirituals," 1925.

JOHNSON, J. ROSMUND, "Negro National Anthem."

WHITE, CLARENCE CAMERON, "Nobody Knows the Trouble I've Seen."